Method in Prayer

An Exposition and Exhortation – The Practice of Praying to God in Petition, Adoration, Confession

By William Graham Scroggie

PANTIANOS
CLASSICS

Published by Pantianos Classics

ISBN-13: 978-1-78987-152-4

First published in 1916

Contents

Preface

By the Right Rev. H. C. G. Moule, D.D.,
Lord Bishop of Durham

THE subject of this book is of supreme importance. The treatment of the subject is worthy of the title. It is a practical illustration throughout of the value of METHOD, in "exposition and exhortation."

The reader is led from one great prayer-topic to another, and from one aspect of that particular topic to another, by sure and measured steps of progress, singularly helpful alike to understanding and to memory — both of which mental actions are as much helped by true method as they are baffled by its absence. Mr. Scroggie's mastery of method extends itself, even to his structure of sentence and phrase, including many (not too many) alliterations, often felicitous in their point.

And the soul of the book, if I may put it so, is the true counterpart of its body. The writer is, beyond mistake, though no one could be more modestly reticent about his experience or attainment, a genuine expert in prayer. He writes as they only can write who really know the way into the Presence, in reverence and in faith, and who, once in it, know what it is to open the soul to its Lord in the precious exercises of adoration, confession, petition, intercession, and thanksgiving, with the purposeful "labour in prayer" which St. Paul loved to see in his dear Epaphras of old. The perusal of the book has been a means of help to my own soul, by way of much searching of heart, and much invaluable suggestion. I trust, and I expect, that it will prove likewise a gain, a guide, and a living stimulus to very many other readers.

May our Lord use it widely, to increase the volume of that mighty implement of power with God and with man, the Prayer of Faith.

Handley Dunelm

Chapter One - The Practice of Prayer

IN that little classic on Prayer, *The Still Hour,* by Dr. Austin Phelps, these words occur: "A consciousness of the absence of God is one of the standard incidents of religious life"; and they are comparatively few in number who will be prepared to challenge that solemn statement. If we who profess to belong to Christ were to make frank confession of our experience in the secret place, we might, perhaps, most fittingly do so in the words of Bishop Hall, "If God had not said, 'Blessed are those that hunger,' I know not what could keep weak Christians from sinking in despair. Many times, all I can do is to complain that I want Him, and wish to recover Him." If this be true of a very large proportion of the people of God, and we fear it is, then, assuredly, we are face to face with the explanation of our flabby faith, and fruitless service. One of the greatest mistakes that a Christian can make is to imagine that increased social or spiritual activity can be any compensation for the lack of secret communion with God. A prayerful life is always a powerful life; and a prayerless life is always a powerless life. If we cannot pray aright, we really can do nothing aright; but how slow we are to believe that. We find a spiritual law at work in the uniform experience that the more we pray, the more we need to, and want to; and the less we pray, the less is the desire to do so. The same thing is true of Bible study, and Christian service. There are very many quite conscious of all this, and desirous that this state of things shall give place to a life of peace, and joy and power in God and with men, but they know not how the change may be brought about.

Well, surely the first thing must be a confession of failure: "We know not what we should pray for, neither how we should pray, as we ought"; and then, with trustful heart we must make request of the Lord, as did the disciples of old, "Lord, teach us to pray." In reply to such confession and request will come the answer, "After this manner therefore pray ye."

It is about the manner or method of prayer that I wish to say a little, in the hope that that which has been of inestimable value in my own life, may prove to be a like blessing in the lives of some others. Of course, prayer is a thing of the spirit, and no method can be of any avail which does not fully recognize that fact. We must pray in the Holy Ghost, with all prayer in the Spirit, Who Himself maketh intercession for us. That is the mystical and fundamental fact, but in order to its becoming a happy and abiding experience with each of us, we must co-operate with the Divine Spirit in ways reasonable and essential. Two of the most important of these are: Time and Method.

Without *time* for prayer, nothing can be accomplished; and yet not unfrequently men excuse or explain their lack of prayerfulness by saying they have not time. There's time for business, time for pleasure, time for social and Christian service, but no time for that exercise which would give to all these, and other things, power and effect.

Daniel prayed three times a day, and David, it would seem, seven times: and we cannot read the Gospels with any care and not be impressed with the fact that our Lord's was a life of communion with the Father.

"Cold mountains and the midnight air
  Witnessed the fervour of His prayer."

The simple fact is, *we must find time* for prayer, or we shall perish: we must regard it to be as essential to our souls as is our dinner daily to our bodies. For every child of God some time each day must be reserved for private communion with Him; and we can better afford to drop anything in the day's programme than that. What time that should be, or how long, no one can judge for another, as circumstances so widely differ; but that there should be some such time, is not a matter of opinion, but an unquestionable necessity. Robert Murray McCheyne has said: "I ought to spend the best hours of the day in communion with God. It is my noblest and most fruitful employment, and is not, therefore, to be thrust into any corner"; and we know from his biography, that it was his habit never to see the face of man until he had seen the face of God. To take time out of prayer to put into service is a bad investment; but on the contrary, if the most of us took a portion of our service-time, and put it into our prayer-time, we should find that the gain was enormous.

But what about those who do give time daily to prayer, and yet derive no appreciable benefit from it; and to whom it is no delight? Dr. Phelps described this experience in a graphic way when he said: "Are there not many 'closet hours' in which the chief feeling of the worshipper is an oppressed consciousness of the absence of reality from his own exercises? He has no words which are, as George Herbert says, 'heart deep.' He not only experiences no ecstasy, but no joy, no peace, no repose. He has no sense of being at home with God. The stillness of the hour is the stillness of a dead calm at sea. The heart rocks monotonously on the surface of the great thought of God, of Christ, of Eternity, of Heaven —

"'As idle as a painted ship
  Upon a painted ocean.'"

That this is actually the experience of many cannot be questioned, neither can we doubt that large numbers of these deeply deplore the fact. But how may it be corrected? How may our quiet time become a supreme joy, to which, through all the hours of the day, we shall look back and for ward? Surely this is God's purpose for us, and surely it is worth any effort to attain.

Assuming the pre-requisites of time, and a heart and mind in adjustment with the will of God, the most important thing in the prayer-life is to have a right *method;* and we are convinced that it is for the lack of this that so many fail, and become discouraged. Our conception of what prayer is, has been pitifully narrow. For the most part, it has been limited to asking things from God, and even within that limitation, the things asked have not been always the highest and best. What we need is a real vision of what prayer is, and such a vision will come to us only as we bring the Bible and our prayer-life into intimate relation. Top long have prayer and Bible study been divorced, and with sad results. What God has joined together, we should never have put asunder. His word to us, and our word to Him are vitally related in His purpose, and must be vitally related in our practice. We are exhorted to "take the Sword of the Spirit, which is the Word of God, praying always with all prayer and supplication in the Spirit," and again, we read of what is "sanctified by the Word of God and prayer." In the Bible God speaks to us; and in prayer wp speak to God: and although it is an instinct of the human soul, apart from revelation, to pray, how to pray can be learnt only from the inspired Word.

The outstanding need of the Church is twofold — a knowledge of God through His Word, and power with Him in prayer. Books simply abound on the subject of prayer, and yet how rare a thing is the effectual practice of it! And why? Are there not two errors of which the people of God stand in danger — the one, -of knowing the Bible intellectually without being concerned to know it experimentally: and the other, of striving after the experimental in prayer either in ignorance or neglect of its mental aspect and requirements? These are opposite errors which should be avoided. One might have an excellent knowledge of the content of Holy Scripture, and at the same time be blind to its divine beauties, and ignorant of its divine power, because his knowledge is of the "letter," and not of the "spirit." In our study of Scripture something more than mental activity is needed, and that is, divine illumination. But when we come to the subject of prayer, this error is generally reversed; that is to say, we look to the Spirit of God for some illumination, some message or vision, apart from the Bible, while we tarry on our knees before Him, with the common result that our thoughts are scattered and slow, and our soul is in a state of perpetual unrest, so that, accomplishing nothing, we become weary, dis appointed, and discouraged, and our prayer-life be comes forced and unnatural.

Is not this state of things to be accounted for in part by the fact that we neglect what may be called the mental means of prayer? Our whole being must enter into the "business" of prayer, and our being is not all "heart"; there are also "mind" and "will." Bishop Hamilton, of Salisbury, used to say that "no man was likely to do much good at prayer who did not begin by looking upon it in the light of a work to be prepared for and persevered in with all the earnestness which we bring to bear upon sub jects which are, in our opinion, at once most interesting and most necessary."

This must mean that our *entire* being is brought into action in the work of prayer; an action which shall far remove us from that sleepy and often sentimental reverie which we are wont to regard as of the nature of true devotion.

The Mind must be at work,

"I will pray with the understanding."

The Heart must be at work,

"My heart panteth after Thee, O God!"

And the Will must be at work,

"I will not let Thee go, except Thou bless me."

And this will be very much the order of action, so far as we may distinguish order in the workings of our souls.

Plainly, then, we must have a mental basis for prayer; upon that the heart's longings will rest, and these the will must keep together and urge until they are satisfied. I fear that it is precisely for lack of such a mental basis that prayer has become to thousands quite a weariness, and an utter failure. But all that may be changed.

We turn, therefore, to the Bible to learn what prayer is, and, also, to make it the medium of our thought and utterance. This latter point is most important, and determines the order of our devotions — not prayer and then the Word, but the Word and then prayer; the former being the medium through which the latter is conceived and expressed. The importance of this is witnessed to by one who knew more about prayer as a practical power than most Christians can claim to know. George Muller, of Bristol, has written thus on the subject —

"It has pleased the Lord to teach me a truth, the benefit of which I have not lost for more than fourteen years. The point is this: I saw more clearly than ever that the first great and primary business to which I ought to attend every day was, to have my soul happy in the Lord. The first thing to be concerned about was not how much I might serve the Lord, or how I might glorify the Lord; but how I might get my soul into a happy state, and how my inner man might be nourished. For I might seek to set the truth before the unconverted, I might seek to benefit believers, I might seek to relieve the distressed, I might in other ways seek to behave myself as it becomes a child of God in this world; and yet, not being happy in the Lord, and not being nourished and strengthened in my inner man day by day, all this might not be attended to in a right spirit. Before this time my practice had been, at least for ten years previously, as an habitual thing, to give myself to prayer after having dressed myself in the morning. Now, I saw that the most important thing I had to do was to give myself to the reading of the Word of God, and to meditation on it, that thus my heart might be comforted, encouraged, warned, re-

8

proved, instructed; and that thus, by means of the Word of God, whilst meditating on it, my heart might be brought into experimental communion with the Lord.

"I began therefore to meditate on the New Testament, from the beginning, early in the morning. The first thing I did, after having asked in a few words the Lord's blessing upon His precious Word, was to begin to meditate on the Word of God, searching as it were into every verse to get blessing out of it; not for the sake of the public ministry of the Word, not for the sake of preaching on what I had meditated upon, but for the sake of obtaining food for my own soul. The result I have found to be almost invariably this, that after a very few minutes my soul has been led to confession, or to thanksgiving, or to intercession, or to supplication; so that, though I did not, as it were, give myself to prayer, but to meditation, yet it turned almost immediately more or less into prayer. When thus I have been for a while making confession or inter cession or supplication, or have given thanks, I go on to the next words or verse, turning all, as I go on, into prayer for myself or others, as the Word may lead to it, but still continually keeping before me that food for my own soul is the object of my meditation. The result of this is, that there is always a good deal of confession, thanksgiving, supplication, or intercession mingled with my meditation, and that my inner man almost invariably is even sensibly nourished and strengthened, and that by breakfast time, with rare exceptions, I am in a peaceful if not happy state of heart. Thus also the Lord is pleased to communicate unto me that which, either very soon after or at a later time, I have found to become food for other believers, though it was not for the sake of the public ministry of the Word that I gave myself to meditation, but for the profit of my own inner man.

"The difference, then, between my former practice and my present one is this: Formerly, when I rose, I began to pray as soon as possible, and generally spent all my time till breakfast in prayer, or almost all the time. At all events I almost invariably began with prayer, except when I felt my soul to be more than usually barren, in which case I read the Word of God for food, or for refreshment, or for a revival and renewal of my inner man, before I gave myself to prayer. But what was the result? I often spent a quarter of an hour, or half an hour, or even an hour, on my knees, before being conscious to myself of having derived comfort, encouragement, and humbling of soul; and often, after having suffered much from wandering of mind for the first ten minutes, or a quarter of an hour, or even half an hour, I only then began really to pray. I scarcely ever suffer now in this way. For my heart being nourished by the truth, being brought into experimental fellow ship with God, I speak to my Father and to my Friend (vile though I am, and unworthy of it) about the things that He has brought before me in His precious Word. It often now astonishes me that I did not sooner see this point. In no book did I ever read about it. No public ministry ever brought the matter before me; no private inter course with a brother stirred me up to this matter."

To go back to the early years of the eighteenth century, we get this word to the same effect from William Law: "When at any time, either reading the Scriptures or any book of Piety, you meet with a passage that more than ordinarily affects your mind, and seems as it were to give your heart a new motion toward God, you should try to turn it into the form of a petition, and then give it a place in your prayers. By this means you would often improve your prayers, and store yourself with proper forms of making the desires of your heart known unto God." And again, returning in another place to the same subject, Law says: "If they were to collect the devotions, confessions, petitions, praises, resignations, and thanksgivings, which are scattered up and down the Psalms, and range them under proper heads, as so much proper fuel for the flame of their own devotions: if their minds were often thus employed, sometimes meditating upon them, sometimes getting them by heart, and making them habitual as their own thoughts, how frequently would they pray who came thus prepared to pray."

But the great classic in illustration of this method is the *Private Devotions* of Lancelot Andrewes, who died in 1626. These *Devotions,* embracing all the elements which unite in prayer considered in its widest aspect, "are filled with all the best passages in the Psalms, in the Prophets, in the Gospels, and in the Epistles, as also in the sermons and litanies and liturgies of the Fathers and the Saints." No work of its kind in the whole range of literature is so perfect an example of what is meant by *praying through the Scriptures,* and a copy of it should be in every Christian home.

Were attention given to this matter the experiences in prayer of thousands of God's children would be transfigured.

What, then, may we say, are those parts, revealed in the Word of God, which go to make the complete idea of prayer? And how may we use the Word in the exercise of those various parts? The answers to these two questions should lead us to a true conception of prayer, and put us in the way of a sound method for the effectual employment of it. Let us, then, attempt to answer these questions.

The complete idea of prayer must always include —

    1. ADORATION, the worship of God:
    2. CONFESSION, the acknowledgment of sin:
    3. PETITION, faith's claim for personal need:
    4. INTERCESSION, the soul's ministry at the throne of grace on behalf of others:
    5. THANKSGIVING, the heart's expression of joy in God.

These ideas are closely related, and yet they must be separately apprehended, and, in some sense, separately put into operation. It will not be possible, of course, rigidly to sever them in the practice of prayer, and yet the distinctions must not be lost sight of. How best these various parts may be balanced in the exercise of prayer, must be discovered by each individual; but, unless one can remain a considerable time in the "secret place," and thus have opportunity to traverse the entire field of devotion, it is well, on the whole, to make one or other of these parts prominent each time one goes aside to meet with God. As a suggestion only, for no hard and fast rule can be made, I would say: Let worship be prominent in the morning, Intercession at mid-day, and Thanksgiving at night; and each time, let the other two circle around these. Such a method would give definiteness and directness to prayer, and, where one was fully surrendered to God, would prove an un failing source of joy and of power.

Let us now examine these five great parts in prayer, and see, also, how we may use the Scriptures in the exercise of them.

Chapter Two – Adoration

THE consideration of one or two things here, will help us immensely, and first —

I. The Idea of Worship

The meaning of the Old Testament word for worship may be gathered from the various translations of it in our versions. In 2 Kings xvii. 36, we read "Him shall ye *worship*": in 2 Sam. ix. 6, "Mephibosheth fell on his face and did (David) *reverence*": in Exod. xi. 8, "All these thy (Pharaoh's) servants *shall bow down themselves* unto me (Moses)": in Gen. xxxvii. 7, "Your sheaves *made obeisance* to my sheaf": in Num. xxii. 31, "Balaam 'fell fiat on his face before the Angel": and in Prov. xii. 25, "Heaviness in the heart of man *maketh it stoop*." All these words have one root idea, that of prostration of oneself before another, or others. When we turn to the New Testament, we meet with a word which graphically reveals the underlying thought of this aspect of prayer. The word uniformly translated "to worship," lays emphasis on the act, rather than on the feeling which prompts the act, and the idea is to be traced to the Greek word for "dog," which seizes upon the characteristic of its fawning, crouching, or crawling at its master's feet. We may say, then, that Divine Worship is an act, wherein the devout soul prostrates itself before God in humble homage and entire submission. Worship so conceived begins, perhaps, in *wonder* which deepens into *reverence,* and is perfected in *love;* so that the worshipful soul can sing —

> "When all Thy mercies, O my God, my rising soul surveys,
>   Transported with the view, I'm lost in wonder, love, and praise."

Where there is this spirit, it will be possible to worship at any time, and anywhere, but the highest experiences of the soul in adoration of God are reserved, surely, for the "still hour," and the "secret place."

We should consider, in the next place —

2. The Object of Worship

The Angel who opened out before the Seer of Patmos such wonderful visions, was mistaken for one divine, but he replied to John, who was about to worship him: "See thou do it not: for I am thy fellow-servant, and of thy brethren the prophets, and of them which keep the sayings of this book: Worship God." God, then, must be the alone Object of our worship. But it is just at this point that difficulty arises in the experience of many. They say, "Yes, God is the Object of worship, but He is Spirit, and seems so unreal, and distant from us. When we kneel before Him, having nothing to appeal to sense, we spend the time in vain endeavours to conceive of Him. How may our Object be known?" Thank God, He has not left us to ourselves in our perplexity, but has given us ways, many and rich, whereby we may know Him, and so, be able to worship Him.

Let us name some of these briefly; and first of all, we may know God —

(i) Through *Nature*. Here His *power* is manifested in creation, His *wisdom* unfolded in adaptation, and His *goodness* displayed in provision for the need of all. True, this revelation is in sufficient and incomplete, yet, with a keener insight, how much more of God we might know by this means. Charles Kingsley felt this, when he said: "The Great Mysticism is the belief which is becoming every day stronger with me, that all symmetrical, natural objects are types of some spiritual truth or existence. When I walk the fields, I am oppressed now and then with an innate feeling that everything I see has a meaning if I could but understand it, and this feeling of being sur rounded with truths, which I cannot grasp, amounts to indescribable awe sometimes. Everything seems to be full of God's reflex, if we could but see it. Oh, how I have prayed to have this mystery un folded at least hereafter! To see, if but for a moment, the whole harmony of the great system, and hear once more the music which the whole universe makes as it performs His bidding." Do not these words recall those others, better known? "The heavens declare the glory of God; and the firmament sheweth His handiwork. Day unto day uttereth speech, and night unto night sheweth knowledge. No speech! No language! Their voice is not heard. Their line is gone out through all the earth, and their words to the end of the world." Verily, "Earth's cramm'd with heaven, and every common bush afire with God." There will, however, be no fear of any one worshipping Nature who has once had a vision of the God of Nature. His works to such will be only His garments, the hem of which they are glad to touch.

But we may also know God —

(ii) Through *Man*. Let us never forget that we were made in God's image and after His like ness, and however these words may ultimately be interpreted, they point to our high origin and holy destiny. While sin has dragged us down from the realization of the divine purpose implied in our creation, God's image in us is not obliterated, though sadly defaced. It has been well said that the.re is no one of God's infinite attributes which 'does not find a shadow in man's soul. A being who can form the idea of Eternity must have some affinity with the Eternal. "Man is not omnipresent, but is there, not a shadow of God's omnipresence in those thoughts of his that roam through space, and find a satisfaction in the contemplation of its boundlessness?" (Orr.) All man's desires, aims, ideals, hopes, and aspirations, in so far as they are good and true, have their source in God: all tenderness, affection, nobility, courage; all sense of the beautiful, and longing after it; all goodness and virtue found in man's nature, and expressed in whatsoever way, are marks of the divine image and proofs of our divine origin:

13

"They are but broken lights of Thee,
  And Thou, O Lord, art more than they."

Should we not, then, as we see these things in one another be led to the worship of Him of Whom they speak, and to the adoring contemplation of Him in Whom all that is humanly and divinely perfect is seen, the last Adam, the Second Man, the Lord from heaven?

But further, we may know God also —

(iii) Through *History.* The writer to the He brews tells us that it is God Who has framed the Ages, Who has built up the Dispensations storey upon storey, and will continue to build them until the House of History is complete. History, it has been said, is His-Story, and we shall never read history aright, whether sacred or profane, until we believe that. But believing it, all history at once takes on a new meaning, and is seen in a new light. "Of Him, and through Him, and to Him are all things." "Of all nations, He hath determined the times before appointed, and the bounds of their habitation." "When the Most High divided to the nations their inheritance, when He separated the sons of Adam, He set the bounds of the peoples according to the number of the children of Israel." Babylon, Persia, Greece, and Rome rose in their time and place according to a divine plan. Not until God's clock struck the hour did Caesar Augustus issue that decree which led to so signal a fulfilment of prophecy. It was not the work of chance that on the eve of the Reformation the printing-press was invented, which was to give the Bible to the whole world; and in an especial sense, to the awakened Church. Look which way we will, this fact stares us in the face, that God is immanent in all history, raising up and casting down, and by means of that which, to the best judgment of men, is such confusion oftentimes, is working out an eternal purpose, and fulfilling an eternal plan. A right view of history, therefore, will give us a new view of God, and must lead us to a truer worship of Him Who is building the Ages.

But God may be known chiefly and finally —

(iv) Through *Christ,* "Who is the effulgence of His glory, and the very image of His substance," and "in Whom dwelleth all the fulness of the God head bodily." It is in Christ that the Infinite has become Local, and that God, who is Spirit, has found an Embodiment. The Divine Son Who existed in the form of God, and counted not the being on an equality with God a thing to be grasped, emptied Himself, taking the form of a bond-slave, being made in the likeness of men, and being found in fashion as a man. God was in Him reconciling the world unto Himself, and God can be fully known only through Him. When we worship Christ, we worship God, for He represents God, and is God. Christ is the Crown of Nature and of Revelation, so that all we find in these is found in Him, all power, wisdom, goodness and love, and He transcends all other revelations of God. He is the Substance of the Bible revelation from its commencement to its close: the Christ of Prophecy in the Old Testament, the

14

Christ of History in the Gospels, the Christ of Experience in the Acts and Epistles, and the Christ of Glory in the Apocalypse.

"Christ is the end, for Christ was the beginning.
Christ the beginning, for the end is Christ."

No man cometh unto the Father but by Him, so that there can be no acceptable worship of God which passes Christ by, for "whosoever denieth the Son, the same hath not the Father." Christ, then, is the way of access to God, and God is worshipped when Christ is worshipped.

Thus far we have seen what is the idea of worship, and that God is the alone Object of worship, revealed, and to be known through Nature, Man, History, and supremely through Christ. Look now, for a moment at —

3. The Character of Worship

Its character is determined by its Object — "God is Spirit, and they that worship Him must worship Him in spirit and in truth." These words are singularly full of meaning, especially when regard is had for the context. "Spirit" points to the essence of Personality, and "Truth" to the essence of Reality: and we may here discern a reference to the Three Persons of the Blessed Trinity — God, to be worshipped; the Spirit acting upon our spirits directing us to worship what is spiritual, and Christ, who is the Truth, furnishing the ground and medium of worship which shall be free from error, and so acceptable to God. Spiritual worship is set over against sensuous worship. Until Christ appeared, God was pleased to help His people in their worship of Him by granting material aids, such as we find in the institutions, offices, and seasons under the Mosaic dispensation: but as all these pointed to Christ, they naturally became invalid after His advent. Meat, and drink, and feast days, Were a shadow of the things to come, "but the body is Christ's."

There is now no longer any need for the Tabernacle or Temple, the Ark, the Altars, the Sacrifices, or the Priests, for the Antitype of all has come, and has brought in the "better" things set out in the Hebrew Epistle. We cannot too strongly insist upon this, that Christ is the fulness of all the shadows, and that there is no longer any need or room for material aids to worship, because we have Him: and the worship which the Father seeks and accepts is that which is "in Spirit." But it must also be "in Truth," that is, true.

If "Spirit" has reference rather to the form, "Truth" has reference, rather to the substance of our worship. We must rightly conceive of Him Whom we worship, so that we may be preserved from what is false or partial. "Judaism (speaking generally) was a worship of the letter and not of the spirit: Samaritanism was a worship of false hood and not of truth. By the Incarnation men are enabled to have immediate communion with God, and thus a worship in spirit has become possible: at the same time the Son is a complete manifestation of God for men, and thus a worship in truth has been placed within our reach" (Westcott). How wonderful that the Father seeketh such as shall worship Him in this way! May we all be found of Him.

There still remains for our consideration —

4. The Means of Worship

These are twofold, the Subjective, or inward means; and the Objective, or outward means,

(i) *The Subjective,* or inward means. Man has heart, and mind, and will, which we speak of as our emotional, intellectual, and volitional faculties, and prayer requires nothing less than the best and fullest use of all these. May be, we have failed in our prayer-life to a large extent in consequence of imagining that it was to be all heart, and that a deliberate effort of mind and will would make it less spiritual. Yet, what saith the Scriptures? "My heart crieth out unto the living God" (Ps. lxxxiv. 2); "I will pray with the *understanding* also" (1 Cor. xiv. 15); "I *will* not let Thee go except Thou bless me" (Gen. xxxii. 26).

Thus are all our powers engaged in this highest of exercises, and all simultaneously. The Heart is set upon the Object, the Mind fastens down upon the facts, and the Will brings both to the work of prayer, and keeps them there. The wor ship of God deserves and demands all our powers, and when we believe this, and act upon it, we shall find our prayer difficulties melting away.

But our faculties alone, though sanctified, are not sufficient. There must be also —

(ii) *The Objective,* or outward means. These are three, answering, in some sense, to our three constitutive faculties just referred to. There is CHRIST, the Determining Means: that is, He is both the limit and the scope of our communion with God. We cannot know more of God than Christ reveals and we need not know less. He determines the field of worship, so to speak. Then, there is the BIBLE, the Evidential Means; being the record of God's full and final revelation of Himself to us. This is the soil in which our faith must take root, and out of which our prayers must ever grow. And finally, there is the SPIRIT, the Illuminating Means; He Who inspired the Word, and Who alone can make us to know its hidden meaning and power. Surely the provision for our prayer-life is more than ample! If our Heart is occupied with Christ, if our Mind is set upon the Word, and if our Will is under the control of the Spirit, we shall be led out into such knowledge and worship of God as shall transfigure all life for us, and shall enable us to live days of heaven upon the earth.

This, then, is the Idea, this the Object, this the Character, and these the Means of all true worship, and at the very foundation of the prayer-life there must be worship, or all will be of no avail with God. How, then, may the worship of God become a present reality and joy in our lives? Only by a true recognition and employment of the ordained Means. Allow me to give one illustration of what is meant.

I enter into my chamber, shut the door, and prepare to worship God. My physical posture does not really signify, whether standing, lying, sitting, or kneeling, for it is not the outward attitude, but the inward spirit which God regards. I at once select a portion of the Scriptures to be the medium, under the direction of the Spirit, of God's unveiling to me, and of my adoration of Him. Let this portion be Rev. i. 13-16. I read it over often enough, silently or audibly, to apprehend the nature of the revelation, and be impressed with its majesty. It is the Son of Man who is set before me, the Object of my worship, as also its End. I con template Him as here revealed, until the glory of His Person, and the majesty of His Office emerge from the text, as mountains from the morning mists. "He is clothed with a garment down to the foot" — What Official Dignity! (Think.) "He is girt about at the breasts with a golden girdle" — What Strong Affection! "His head and His hair are white as white wool, white as snow" — What Perfect Holiness! "His eyes are as a flame, of fire" — What Consuming Knowledge! (Think.) "His feet are like unto burnished brass, as if it had been refined in a furnace" — What Righteous Judgment! "His voice is as the sound of many waters" — What Absolute Authority! (Listen.) "He has in His right hand seven stars" — What Sovereign Administration! "Out of His mouth proceeds a sharp two-edged sword" — What All Searching Truth! "His countenance is as the sun shineth in his strength" — What Transcendent Glory! (Think.) Son of Man, Son of God — in the midst — the Living One — once crucified — now alive for ever and ever — and holding the keys of Death and of Hades — Blessed art Thou for ever and ever — alone worthy to receive power, and riches, and wisdom, and strength, and honour, and glory, and blessing — we adore Thee. For years my soul has dwelt in this marvelous passage, and the Bible is full of such; and those portions which you use and come to know in the way of prayer are of all others most precious to you, because they become part of you. Shall we not put this method to the test, and so find the highway to the Throne of Grace!

An Act of Adoration

By Lancelot Andrewes

> Through the tender mercy of our God the dayspring from
>   on high hath visited us.
> Glory be to Thee, O Lord, glory to Thee,
> Creator of the light, Enlightener of the world.
> God is the Lord, Who hath shewed us light:
>   bind the sacrifice with cords,
>   even unto the horns of the altar.
> Glory be to Thee for the visible light:
> the sun's radiance, the flame of fire;
> day and night, evening and morning;
> for the light invisible and intellectual:
> that which may be known of God,

17

that which is written in the law,
    oracles of prophets,
    melody of psalms,
    instruction of proverbs,
    experience of histories,
    a light which never sets.
By Thy resurrection raise us up unto newness of life,
    supplying to us frames of repentance.
The God of Peace, that brought again from the dead our
    Lord Jesus,
that great Shepherd of the sheep,
through the blood of the everlasting covenant,
Make us perfect in every good work to do His will,
    working in us that which is well pleasing in His sight,
    through Jesus Christ;
    to Whom be glory, for ever and ever.

Chapter Three - Confession

IN the development of Prayer we place Confession next to Adoration, because in practice, the one naturally and necessarily arises out of the other. It will be well then to obtain, at the outset, a true conception of what is meant by Confession. The use of the word in Scripture, together with illustrations therefrom, and elsewhere, must be our guides. So consider —

1. The Meaning of Confession

A variety of ideas unite in this one, such, for instance, as candidness, definiteness, openness, truthfulness, and submissiveness. In the Old Testament, the prevailing thought in Confession is that of praise and thanksgiving, but the root idea, Gesenius tells us, is to show, or point out with the hand extended, hence to profess or confess. When we turn over to the New Testament we find again that the root idea is somewhat remote from the meaning we commonly attach to Confession; yet, upon reflection, we see how true is the connection. The Greek word *homologeo* means to *say the same,* from which comes the ideas, to agree, to admit, to grant, to recognize, to acknowledge, to confess. It will readily be seen that the root idea of the word in each Testament is one and the same, and that the simplest conception of it is expressed by our word *acknowledge.* Confession, therefore, in its widest aspect may mean to give thanks (Heb. xiii. 15), to admit (John i. 20), to recognize (Acts xxiii. 8), to publicly acknowledge (John ix. 22), or to confess sins (1 John i. 9). The thing to apprehend is that, in Confession is the idea of *an objective fact or standard, which acts as a subjective test.* Apply that thought to all the passages referred to above, or any others, and the idea will be plain. It is, however, the last of those meanings of the word that we have in view more particularly here, that is, confession in relation to sin. This will lead us to speak a little about —

2. The Habit of Confession

We have already said that prayer is something to be practised, that it must be cultivated, that the soul must be put under severe discipline in the school of God, else the flesh will triumph. If this discipline begins at worship, at the contemplation and adoration of God, it will inevitably turn to confession of sin, for we can know ourselves only as we know God, Whose holiness is a blazing background, showing up the blackness of our sin. This was the experience of Isaiah, who "saw the Lord sitting upon a throne, high and lifted up, and His train filled the temple . . . and the Seraphim cried one unto another and said, 'Holy, Holy, Holy is the Lord of Hosts; the whole earth is full of His

glory.'" Then said he, "Woe is me, for I am undone: because I am a man of un
clean lips...for mine eyes have seen the King, the Lord of Hosts." It was also
the experience of Israel, who after the delivery of the Decalogue, and when
they saw the thunderings, and the lightnings, and the noise of the trumpet,
and the mountain smoking — removed and stood afar off. And they said unto
Moses: "Speak thou with us, and we will hear: but let not God speak with us,
lest we die." And this has been the experience of saints throughout the ages,
who, the nearer they have gotten to God, have the more keenly been conscious of their sin and unworthiness. We shall do well, then, to think much of -

(i) The Need of Confession. This is abiding. There never will come a time,
in this life, when in the experience of any child of God, there will be no need
to confess sin, and if any have thought that such a time has come to him, or
her, that thought itself is a sin to be confessed. Inadequate views of what sin
is, lie at the bottom of much of the false teaching which is abroad, as, also,
they ac count for the prevailing lack of spirituality on the part of God's people. About positive sins there can be no doubt, sins characterized by the
Psalmist as "presumptuous": evil words and deeds without, and evil imagina-
tions and desires within. Many are the terms employed in Scripture to set
forth the manifoldness of sin, such, for example, as wrong, mischief, guilt,
travail, transgression, evil, rebellion, iniquity, wickedness, vanity, fault,,
breach of trust, disobedience, ignorance, discord, and many more; and it is
only as we come to know what God has said about these things that we can
form any true idea of the real nature of sin.

But the Psalmist speaks also of "secret" sins, by which we are to understand, not sins committed in secret, but sins which we have not consciously
committed, sins of ignorance, sins "hidden" from us (Lev. v. 3-4). That such
there are beyond all reckoning, is implied in a striking passage in John's First
Epistle: "If we walk in the light as He is in the light, ...the blood of Jesus Christ
His Son cleanseth us from all sin." Manifestly, walking with God in the light
pre-supposes the absence of all positive sin, and yet there is the unceasing
need of the blood for cleansing, implying the presence of that from which we
need to be cleansed. Revelation and experience answer to one another here,
revelation declaring the fact, and experience witnessing to it. Any soul that is
growing in spiritual stature can testify that things which to him were right a
few years ago, he now sees perhaps to be wrong. But it is he who has
changed, and not the things; with a quickened sense of God has come a
quickened consciousness of sin; and the keener of scent we become in the
fear of the Lord, the more sensitive will we be to the presence or approach of
sin. Hence, the appeal of these familiar words —

"Search all my sense, and know my heart
    Who only canst make known,
  And let the deep, the *hidden* part
    To me be fully shown.
  Throw light into the darkened cells,

20

Where passion reigns within;
Quicken my conscience till it feels
The loathsomeness of sin."

We need to pray daily for a truer sense of sin, or, for a truer sense of what holiness is, for it is in the presence of divine holiness that sin stands most fully revealed. Conviction, therefore, must precede and accompany confession. It was not until the prodigal "came to himself," that he said, "I have sinned": and it was not until "David's heart smote him after that he had numbered the people," that he said to the Lord, "I have sinned greatly in that I have done."

The one thing which can put and keep God at a distance from the soul is sin unconfessed. "I will go and return to My place, till they acknowledge their offence, and seek My face."

But there are many, we believe, who are conscious of the abiding need of Confession, who feel they do not get satisfaction in the act. This may be because attention has not been given to what God requires of us. So let us think for a moment of—

(ii) The Act of Confession. After setting forth the sins of the children of Israel, and indicating what judgments were impending, Hosea says, *"Take with you words,* and turn to the Lord: say unto Him, Take away all iniquity, and receive us graciously." Oh how difficult it is to give expression in words to the sorrow of our hearts for sin; they are upon our lips as burning coals; and the sound of them fills us with shame. Yet, so it must be; and it is well that it should be so, until we are shamed out of our sinning. Definite sin must be definitely confessed: a general, or summary confession is not enough. In that piercing cry of David's after his terrible fall, the sin of which he had been guilty was definitely confessed. He says to the Lord, "My transgression, mine iniquity, my sin, this evil, blood-guiltiness."

Equally specific were Ezra (ix.), Nehemiah (ix.), and Daniel (ix.), in their great confessions; and so must it be with us, until, as they, we can say: "O my God, I am ashamed and blush to lift up my face unto Thee, my God: for our iniquities have increased over our head, and our trespass is grown up unto the heavens."

And confession must not only be *definite,* but *full,* nothing must be kept back or concealed. Aaron of old had to lay both his hands on the head of the live goat, "and confess over him *all* the iniquities of the children of Israel, and *all* their transgressions in all their sins"; for perfect cleansing comes only upon full confession. And, needless to say, confession, definite and full, must always be *real.* God knows the state of our minds, and however we ex press ourselves, our confession is acceptable to Him if it is the utterance of a broken and a contrite heart, which He will never despise.

Conviction, Sorrow, Repentance, Confession, and Conversion are vitally related to one another. There may be conviction without sorrow, or conviction and sorrow without repentance. It is this fact which led the Apostle to thank God that the Corinthians "sorrowed unto repentance," a repentance which issued in confession and conversion.

David said, "I will be sorry for my sin"; and Solomon carried on the thought when he said, "Whoso confesseth and forsaketh his sins shall have mercy."

Lancelot Andrewes, Bishop of Winchester, in the time of James I. (already referred to) has left in his *Private Devotions* some incomparable examples of the true spirit of confession. Perhaps the most wonderful is that which is given at the end of this chapter, and it will be better understood the more we know of the influences that were brought to bear upon him at the Court of the King.

Of that out-breaking of heart, almost too sacred for the public eye, Dr. Alexander Whyte has said: "If ever God got at the hands of a sinful man a sacrifice that satisfied Him, and made Him say on the spot, 'Bring forth the best robe,' it was surely in Lancelot Andrewes's closet, and after that great Act of Confession."

With that prayer should be read, almost daily, the great Penitential Psalms, which have been the language of the people of God for over twenty-eight centuries, and will continue to be the vehicle of our confessions to the end of time.

"Wash me thoroughly from my iniquity,
　And cleanse me from my sin.
　For I acknowledge my transgressions;
　And my sin is ever before me,
　Create in me a clean heart, O God;
　And renew a right spirit within me.
　Restore unto me the joy of Thy salvation;
　And uphold me with Thy free Spirit."

"When I kept silence, my bones waxed old,
　Through my roaring all the day long.
　For the day and night Thy hand was heavy upon me;
　My moistness is turned into the drought of summer.
　I acknowledged my sin unto Thee,
　And mine iniquity have I not hid.
　I said,
　I will confess my transgressions unto the Lord;
　And Thou forgavest the iniquity of my sin."

"O Lord, rebuke me not in Thy wrath;
　Neither chasten me in Thy hot displeasure.
　For mine iniquities have gone over mine head:
　As an heavy burden they are too heavy for me.
　I am troubled; I am bowed down greatly;
　I go mourning all the day long.
　My heart panteth, my strength faileth me:
　As for the light of mine eyes,

It also is gone from me.
In Thee, O Lord, do I hope:
Thou wilt hear, O Lord my God.
I will declare mine iniquity:
I will be sorry for my sin.
Forsake me not, O Lord:
O my God, be not far from me,
Make haste to help me, O Lord, my Salvation."

"Out of the depths have I cried unto Thee, O Lord.
Lord, hear my voice:
Let Thine ears be attentive to the voice of my supplications.
If Thou, Lord, shouldest mark iniquities,
O Lord, who shall stand?
But there is forgiveness with Thee,
That Thou mayest be feared.
I wait for the Lord, my soul doth wait,
And in His word do I hope.
My soul waiteth for the Lord
More than they that watch for the morning:
I say, more than they that watch for the morning."

As in the case of Worship so here, the Scriptures should be the medium of our thought and utterance. The out-pouring of the confession and longings of such men as Job, Moses, Samuel, David, Hezekiah, Ezra, Nehemiah, Daniel, and Paul is not the least precious part of the Church's heritage in those great souls; and to these must be added the exalted, because heartbroken utterances of the great saints of all the ages.

Perhaps some one will object that the language of confession, and of prayer generally must be one's own, and not another's, and that in the use of litanies one is prone to become mechanical, and to lose the real sense of the presence of God. No one, of course, can prescribe forms of prayer for another, or say what is best suited to the need of others; but if we believe that the prayers which have been preserved through the ages were directed by the Spirit of God in those who first uttered them, surely, in so far as they truly express our experience, and attitude of soul, they may be used to give expression to our desires.

A word or two must be said about —

3. The Fruits of Confession

These are spiritual and ethical and not the one without the other.

(i) The Spiritual fruits are, (a) Forgiveness; and (b) Cleansing. The former being related to the righteousness of God, and the latter to His holiness. We are apt to confuse these two things, and regard them as one, yet they are sharply distinguished in Scripture. "If we confess our sins, He is faithful and just to *forgive* us our sins, and *to cleanse* us from all unrighteousness." Confession, Forgiveness, and Cleansing — these should always be distinguished, yet never separated. Perhaps a simple illustration will be helpful. A young child is prettily dressed in a new white frock, in readiness for a party, and is told by mother not to go out into the street to play, lest she should get dirty. But the little girl sees some of her friends making mud castles by the kerbstone, and, of course, that was too great an attraction, so out she goes and joins them. In the course of play her new clean frock becomes all bespattered with mud. She suddenly awakes to the fact, and her conscience smites her. With tearful face she runs to her mother, confesses her dis obedience, and asks her forgiveness, which is freely bestowed. But what about the frock? Does the mother's forgiveness make that clean? Oh, no, you say, that must be washed. True, and the remembrance of the wrong of disobedience is not put completely away until the frock is washed. And so it is with us all. "If we *confess* our sins, He is faithful and just to forgive us our sins, and to *cleanse* us from all unrighteousness." Through Christ Jesus our forgiveness satisfies the righteous ness of God, but our cleansing satisfies His holiness.

But there are beyond this —

(ii) The Ethical Fruits of Confession. These also are twofold: (*a*) Restitution and Compensation, on the one hand; and (*b*) Jealousy of further lapse, on the other hand. Nothing could be plainer than the teaching of Scripture on the first point. We read that he who has sinned and is guilty "shall restore that which he took violently away, or the thing which he hath deceitfully gotten, or that which was delivered him to keep, or the lost thing which he found, or all that about which he hath sworn falsely: he shall even restore it in the principle, *and shall add the fifth part more thereto,* and give it unto him to whom it appertained, in the day of his trespass offering" (Lev. vi. 4-5; see also, ch. v. 16; Num. v. 6-7; Matt. v. 23-24). Restitution is not enough, there must be compensation. An awakened conscience will at once respond to this, as in the case of Zacchaeus, who said, "If I have taken anything from any man by false accusation, I restore fourfold." The publican rose to a much higher standard than the Old Testament law required. And so did a little girl at a mission I once conducted. There were about thirteen of a family, and they all professed Christ but this child of about nine years. After the service one night, her mother asked her why she had not gone into the inquiry room, and this was the substance of her reply: "Mother, the preacher told us that if we had robbed any one we had to restore fourfold if we wanted the forgiveness of God. A long time ago, Mother, you sent me up to your bedroom for something, and I saw in a drawer three-halfpence, which I took, and no one knew anything about it: so before I ask God's forgive ness, I want to ask yours, and give you my only sixpence, which according to the preacher will be a fourfold return." And my dear little friend accepted Christ as her Saviour the next night. If all who profess the Name of our Lord were as sensitive as she, what a clearing there would be of consciences, and what an adjustment of wrongs and robberies, which too often stalk about in the guise of *business.*

24

But where confession has been made, forgive ness and cleansing received, and restitution made, there will be great jealousy of further lapse, as in the case of the Corinthians: "For behold this self-same thing, that ye sorrowed after a godly sort, what carefulness it wrought in you, yea, what clearing of yourselves, yea, what indignation, yea, what fear, yea, what vehement desire, yea, what zeal, yea, what revenge! In all things ye have approved yourselves to be clear in this matter" (2 Cor. vii. ii).

This is one of the great values of true confession, it shames us out of our sin, and makes us jealous for the honour and glory of God. Shall we not then take with us words and say: "Come, and let us return unto the Lord: for He hath torn, and He will heal us; He hath smitten, and He will bind us up. After two days will He revive us: in the third day He will raise us up, and we shall live in His sight. Then shall we know, if we follow on to know the Lord: His going forth is prepared as the morning; and He shall come unto us as the rain, as the latter and former rain unto the earth."

An Act of Confession

By Lancelot Andrewes

"O God, Thou knowest my foolishness, and my sins are not hid from Thee. I acknowledge my transgressions, and my sin is ever before me. I cover not my transgressions, like Adam; nor do I incline my heart to words of wicked ness, to make excuses for my sins. I will confess my transgressions unto the Lord, and all that is within me and all my bones shall say, I have sinned, I have sinned against Thee; I have gone astray, like a sheep that is lost; I have been perverse, as a bull-ock unaccustomed to the yoke; I have returned to folly as a dog returneth to his vomit: as a sow that was washed to her wallowing in the mire. I give glory to Thee, Lord, and make confession that I have sinned; and thus and thus have I done.

Lord, break not the bruised reed; quench not the smoking flax; let not the wa-terflood overflow me, neither let the deep swallow me up, and let not the pit shut her mouth upon me.

Lord, all my desire is before Thee, and my groaning is not hid from Thee. Thou knowest, Lord, that I say the truth, in Christ, and lie not, my conscience also bear-ing me witness in the Holy Spirit, that I have great heaviness and continual sor-row in my heart because I have thus sinned against Thee; that I am a burden to myself, in that I cannot sorrow more; that I beseech from Thee a contrite heart, groanings that cannot be uttered, tears of blood. Woe is me for my leanness, for the hardness of my heart, for the dryness of my eyes, Lord, I repent; I repent, O Lord; help Thou mine impenitence, and more and still more bruise, and wound, and pierce, and strike my heart.

Behold, O Lord, that I am indignant with myself on account of the foolish and vain and mischievous and perilous desires of my flesh; that I abhor myself for the madness and baseness and vileness of those desires; worthy of con fusion and reproach; that my confusion is continually before me, and the shame of my face hath covered me. Woe is me, that I did not reverence nor dread the incomprehensibleness of The Glory, The Tremendous Power, The Awfulness of the Presence, The Strict Justice, The Gentle Goodness. How have I been drawn away by mine own lusts; how have I hated reproof, and have not obeyed the voice of my teachers.

Behold, O Lord, that fearfulness and trembling are come upon me, and the terrors of death are fallen upon me. What fear, what trembling, what terror, what agony, what extremity, have I yet to see; what confusion will seize me; what shades will surround me! How terrible is Thy judgment seat, O God, when the thrones are set and the angels in presence, and men brought in, and the books opened, and the works investigated, and the thoughts scrutinized, and the hidden things of darkness made known. What will be the judgment against me? When there is the incorruptible Judge, and the tremendous tribunal, and the excuseless defence, and the irrefragable accusation, and the fearful punishment, and the eternal Gehenna, and the pitiless angels, and the open hell-mouth, and the roaring river of fire, and that fire inextinguishable, and the prison of darkness, and that darkness rayless, and the bed of live coals, and the restless worm, and the indissoluble chains, and the immeasurable chaos, and the wall that cannot be passed, and the lament that cannot be consoled, and none to assist, to advocate, to free.

Behold, O Lord, I adjudge myself worthy of, and amen able to, and guilty of, eternal punishment, yea, and all the straits of this world. From Thee, O Lord, I have merited death, from Thee, the Just One, but yet to Thee, O Lord, I appeal to Thee, the Merciful One: from the tribunal of justice to the mercy seat of grace; permit, O Lord, this appeal; if Thou dost not, we perish. And, O Lord, carest Thou not that we perish? Thou Who wilt have all men to be saved, Who art not willing that any should perish.

Behold me, O Lord, self-condemned.

Behold me; and enter not Thou, O Lord, into judgment with Thy servant. I am less than the least of all Thy mercies; I am not worthy to be made even the lowest of Thy hired servants; I am not worthy to gather the crumbs that fall from Thy table; I am not worthy to touch the hem of Thy garment. And now, O Lord, humbling myself under Thy mighty hand, I bow my knees to Thee, and fall down to the ground, on my face. I stretch forth my hands unto Thee; my soul thirsteth after Thee, as a thirsty land. I dare not lift up as much as mine eyes unto heaven, but smite upon my breast. Out of the depths hath my soul cried unto Thee, and all that is within me.

For Thy great mercy, for the multitude of Thy tender mercies, for Thy Name's sake, for the Glory of Thy Name, be merciful to my sin; for it is great, it is exceeding great.

For the multitude, the great multitude, the riches, the abundance, the superabundance of Thy tender mercies, be merciful unto me, unto me, O Lord, unto me. Lord, O Lord, be merciful unto me, chief of sinners. Lord, let Thy mercy rejoice against Thy judgment, in my sins. O my Lord, where my sin hath abounded, there let Thy grace more exceedingly abound. O Lord, hear; O Lord, forgive; O Lord, hearken and do; defer not; for Thine own sake, O my God."

Chapter Four – Petition

IN the unfolding of the subject of Prayer, we come to Supplication, or Petition, by which is meant *prayer for oneself* as distinguished from intercession, which is prayer for others. This naturally follows Worship and Confession, for, if the revelation of God to our hearts in Worship leads us to Confession of sin and need, in Petition we shall at once make appeal for the supply of that personal need, and claim for ourselves the divine provision. If the two former aspects of prayer are a necessary preparation for Petition, this last is in turn a preparation for the two aspects which are to follow, Intercession and Thanksgiving; so that all these parts are vitally related to one another. Bearing in mind, then, that we are now considering prayer in relation to our own personal need, let us think first of all of —

1. The Warrant for Offering Our Petitions

Of the many passages which encourage us to come to our loving Father and tell Him all that is in our heart, one or two must suffice here. In Heb. iv. 1 6, we read, "Come boldly unto the throne of grace, that we may obtain mercy and find grace to help in time of need." Every word in this verse is significant. "Come," that is one of the greatest, as it is one of the simplest, words in the Bible. "Boldly," that is, with courage, candor, and confidence. "To the throne of grace," which is none other than the throne of the divine government, and from which there can be no appeal, as there is nothing higher. "That we may obtain mercy," a clear reference to our need in view of the *past,* and suggestive of the atoning merits (mercy) and the claim of faith (obtain). "And find grace to help in time of need." This has reference to *future* need, and is suggestive of the storing of grace against the time when it will be, in specific ways, required. To this great call to prayer, add such passages as: "Ask, and it shall be given you; seek, and ye shall find; knock, and it shall be opened unto you"; and, "Be careful for nothing; but in everything by prayer and supplication, with thanks giving, let your requests be made known to God," and we are in possession of warrant sufficient for spreading out before Him all the desire of our hearts. In the light of these passages, our right of way to the throne of grace can never be effectually challenged; and yet how few, comparatively, utilize this charter of liberty and privilege. The Spirit of God says, "Come — come — come," and He Himself shows us the way. How is it then that so few do come? This will lead us to consider —

2. The Conditions of Prevailing Prayer

God may not be approached anyhow and by anybody. The divine promises to those who would pray, rest upon the fulfilment of certain conditions, to neglect which is to render the promises void. This fact, so clear and reasonable, is one which, for the most part, we either do not know, or will not believe; for we find everywhere the most flagrant disregard of these conditions. Let us recite a few of them.

(i) We must have Confidence in Prayer as a Practical Power (Heb. xi. 6), otherwise we are simply beating the air, or pouring water through a sieve when we pray. If we do not believe that prayer changes things, then, in the interests of honesty, let us abandon it. Dr. Schauffler has well said —

"Prayer is either a prodigious *force*, or a disgraceful *farce*. If a *farce,* you may pray much, and get little; if a *force,* you may pray little and get much." Faith is absolutely essential to effectuality; we must "believe God answers prayer, answers always, everywhere," if we would accomplish anything in the world.

(ii) We must be Frank and Earnest in the presence of God (Matt. vii. 7). Is there some thing you need? Ask for it. The Apostle James says, "Ye have not because ye ask not." It is of the very essence of prayer to ask, and answers are the reward only of such as do. And our asking must not be casual but constant; not indifferent, but intense. "Ask — seek — knock." If asking does not avail, then seek, and if seeking proves ineffective, then knock. Singularly enough, the initial letters of these words spell ASK, as though to remind us of this primary necessity, and to assure us that "He is a rewarder of them that diligently seek Him."

(iii) We must be always Definite in our requests (Matt. vii. 9-11). Indefinite petitions can hardly expect more than indefinite answers: if we are vague with God, He will be vague with us: but He has promised to give good things to them that ask Him. A glance at the passage before us will reveal that those "good things" are in two categories; first, necessities such as "bread"; and next, luxuries, such as "fish." It is not our Father's way to keep His children on dry bread, and He has encouraged us to ask for more than the bare necessities of life. But we must be definite with Him. Generalities in prayer are only a refuge for unbelief.

(iv) We must offer our petitions to God in Faith (Mark xi. 24). This is a remarkable passage, the point of which is too often overlooked. Whatsoever things we desire when we pray, we are to believe that we do, at the time, receive them, and in God's good time we shall receive them; in other words, we are to receive the thing in order to get it. A secretary of the Sunday School Union, addressing a gathering of children, asked a somewhat difficult question, which a small lad promptly answered. Said the teacher: "If that lad will come to me at the close of the meeting, and give me his name and address, I will send him a book from headquarters when I get back to-morrow." The lad, of course, fulfilled the condition, and then bounded off home and shouted, "Mother, I've got a book," and when she asked "Where is it?" he replied, "I haven't got it." There is the entire secret in a nutshell. If we fulfil the condition of prayer, we may at once, by faith in God's Word, receive the promises, and when the time comes those promises will materialize. This is no pious idea, but a practical reality which I have proved in my own prayer-life. I was once in need of eight pounds fifteen shillings with which to pay my house-rent, which fell due in a week from the time of which I speak, and I had nothing in hand for the need. I took the above text to God at one o'clock that day, and in faith received the money from Him; and upon reaching home a few hours later I found the following letter awaiting me:

"Dear Mr. Scroggie, — Kindly accept the enclosed from the Lord through me," and a cheque for ten pounds accompanied. Upon inquiry I learned that the donor left the letter at my house at the precise hour in which I had cast myself upon the Word of God. Faith laying hold of the promises is invincible, and is the mightiest power entrusted to man. Let me name one other condition only —

(v) We must ask according to the Will of God (1 John v. 14). "This is the confidence that we have in Him, that if we ask anything according to His will, He heareth us; and if we know that He hears us, whatsoever we ask, we know that we have the petitions that we desired of Him." That is one of the profoundest passages on prayer in the whole range of Scripture, because it goes right to the heart of the matter. But the problem with thousands of the Lord's people is to know what is the will of God; and we are constantly asked, "How can one know?" Perhaps another verse in this Epistle will help to resolve that difficulty. In chapter iii. 22, we read, "Whatsoever we ask, we receive of Him, because we keep His commandments, and do those things that are pleasing in His sight." If we do the will of God, we shall know it, for every step taken in obedience to His word lets loose fresh light, and secures to us fuller liberty. But in addition to obedience to the divine commands, there should be a devout consideration and anticipation of what would give Christ pleasure. The sweetness of home does not consist in obedience to the rules of the house, but in the manifestation of love on the part of the family, each studying the other's comfort and pleasure, and delighting to make provision for it. And so it is in the highest relationship. There are many things that Christ will not command us to do, which He expects us, out of love for Himself, to do; and these are "the things that are pleasing in His sight." If we are living thus close to Him, we shall know by a certain spiritual intuition what His will for us is, at any given time, and if in prayer we claim the fulfilment of that will, it shall be done. If we abide in Him, and His words abide in us, we may ask what we will, and it shall be done unto us. There is an unlimited promise resting on a limited condition, and we may take it at its face value. But if we are not abiding in Him, and if His word is not abiding in us, we cannot, of course, know what His will for us is, and so cannot pray aright. There are very many more conditions of prevailing prayer which should be sought out and responded to, but these may serve just to blaze the way.

But we should search out also —

3. The Promises Made to Him Who Prays

It cannot be too strongly insisted upon, that the divine precepts and promises go together. If we observe the precepts, God will fulfil the promises; if we meet the conditions, God is responsible for the rest: but if we neglect our part, we have left to us no ground of expectation that prayer will ever rise higher than the ceiling.

How many and magnificent are the promises which God has made to those who draw near to Him as humble and trustful suppliants. It has been pointed out that all the unconditioned phrases are applied to prayer: "whosoever," "whatsoever," "wheresoever," "whensoever," "all," "any," "every"; that no one should be left in doubt as to the large ness of the divine heart, or the readiness of the divine will. James III. of Scotland said to his prisoner, Ayliffe, who stood before him, "You know it is in my power to pardon you?" "Yes," he replied, "I know it is in your power, but it is not in your nature." But when we come to Him who is King of kings, we find that "His love is as great as His power, and knows neither measure nor end." As we enter the secret place we hear Him say, "I will establish My covenant with you." "I will bless thee." "I will make thee exceeding fruitful." "I will go down with thee into Egypt; and I will surely bring thee up again." "I will nourish you and your little ones." "I will put thee in a cleft of a rock!" "I will give thee counsel." "I will do to thee all that thou requirest." "I will restore health unto thee." "I will build thee, and thou shalt be built." "I will pardon all your iniquities." "I will go before thee, and will direct all thy ways." "I will help thee, saith the Lord." "I will be your God." "I will never leave thee, nor forsake thee." These promises, and hundreds besides, are ours, frankly to claim, and freely to enjoy: they are as so many easy chairs in which we may settle down and be at rest, remembering that all the divine promises are "yea" and "amen" in Christ Jesus. When the Lord threatened to destroy Israel in consequence of their sin at Mount Sinai, Moses reminded Him of His covenant with Abram, and claimed the fulfilment of it; and, we read, "the Lord repented of the evil which He thought to do unto the people." It is said also of Luther that he would put his finger on a promise and say, "Now, Lord, if Thou dost not fulfil that promise to me, I will never trust Thee again." This may sound very bold and irreverent, but the spirit of it is such as the Lord delights to honor, for He is never better pleased than when we take Him at His word.

It is important also to understand what are —

4. The Proper Subjects for Daily Prayer

One passage of Scripture will suffice to guide us in this matter. "Seek ye first the kingdom of God, and His righteousness, and all these things shall be added unto you" (Matt. vi. 33). Two classes of things are referred to: things spiritual, and things temporal. Not the spiritual only, and not the temporal first. Our gracious Father has made provision for the whole of our need, but there is a priority of some things over others. Our spiritual need is our supreme need, because our souls are of more consequence than our bodies;

30

and yet, in our prayers, we give more attention to the latter than to the former. Have you ever studied the prayers of the Apostle Paul, of which there are not a few? Perhaps the most interesting feature of them is their intense spirituality. What he is concerned about is that he may have the spirit of wisdom and revelation in the knowledge of Christ; that the eyes of his heart might be enlightened; that he might know what was the issue of his holy calling, and what the riches of the glory of Christ's inheritance in him and all the saints, and how exceeding great is His power towards and in those who believe (Eph. i). He longs also to be strengthened with might, by the Holy Spirit, in the inner man: to be rooted and grounded in love, and to apprehend what is the breadth, and length, and depth, and height of the divine love, which he is conscious must transcend all human knowledge (Eph. iii.). On this high plane also are his prayers in Philippians and Colossians and the two Thessalonians. Truly he observed the word of Christ to "seek first the kingdom of God, and His righteousness." But he was not above seeking the other things, for many references in his Epistles reveal that he took all his temporal need also to God, and asked counsel of Him concerning his daily movements and supplies. The following will suffice to illustrate this: "I besought the Lord thrice that it" [his thorn in the flesh] "might depart from me." "Making request, if by any means now at length I might have a prosperous journey by the will of God to come unto you." "I rejoiced in the Lord greatly that now at the last your care of me hath flourished again" [when money was sent]. "Pray that I may be delivered from unreasonable and wicked men." And the Apostle's testimony is that sometimes he had much and sometimes little, sometimes he was full and sometimes destitute, but that Christ was his blessed sufficiency always. God has not promised to supply all our "wants," but He has undertaken the provision of our "needs," and has guaranteed that "no good thing will He withhold from them that walk uprightly."

Tell God, therefore, all you need, spiritual and temporal, and rest assured that He Who is so careful with our souls will not be careless about our bodies. It will be of immense help to keep a prayer diary that the perspective and progress of our prayers may be examined from time to time.

One other thing, in this short study, claims our attention, namely —

5. The Practical Outcome of Our Requests

Does God answer prayer? Surely that is a proper subject of inquiry, and one to which every Christian should be able to give an unhesitating answer. Of course God answers prayer; and if the testimonies of all His people throughout the ages were to be written, in the language of St. John, "I suppose that even the world itself could not contain the books that should be written." Abram and Moses, and David, and Elijah and Daniel, and Paul got their prayers answered, and so may you and I. The God of George Muller is our God also, and will honor our obedience and faith, as He honored his.

But we may hold much too narrow an idea as to what constitutes an answer to prayer. This subject receives ample illustration in the fifth chapter of Mark's Gospel, where three prayers are answered, but all differently. First, there is the prayer of the demons, to be allowed to go into the. swine. Then, the prayer of the healed man, to be allowed to accompany Jesus. And finally, the prayer of Jairus, that Jesus would come and heal his daughter. In each of these we must distinguish between the *petition* and the *desire*. In the first case, the petition was answered, and the desire unanswered. The demons desired a place of safety, but in getting their petition answered, they lost their desire. In the second case, the desire was answered, and the petition unanswered. The healed man desired to express his gratitude to Jesus, and thought that by accompanying Him he would be doing so; but his gratitude had to find expression in another way, "Go...tell." His desire was granted. In the third case, both desire and petition were answered. Jairus wanted his daughter to be restored, and so asked Jesus to come to his house and raise her up; and Jesus did both. So in our prayers, often times when the terms of request are denied, the desire of our heart is granted, as, when Saul cried, "What will Thou have me to do?" the reply was made, "I will show him how great things he must suffer."

History is not without illustration also, of desire being unheeded in the granting of petitions. We read of Israel that, "He gave them their request, but sent leanness into their soul." God in His mercy neglects the terms of many of our prayers, because He sees how injurious to us would be the fulfilment. And then, again, the truer our prayers are, the nearer will the correspondence be between the desire of the heart, and the request of the lips, so that Christ may answer both.

An Act of Petition

By Lancelot Andrewes

The power of the Father guide me,
the wisdom of the Son enlighten me,
the working of the Spirit quicken me.
> Guard Thou my soul,
> strengthen my body,
> elevate my senses,
> direct my course,
> order my habits,
> shape my character,
> bless my actions,
> fulfil my prayers,
> inspire holy thoughts,
> pardon the past,
> correct the present,
> prevent the future.

Now unto Him that is able to do exceeding abundantly above all that we ask or think, according to the power that worketh in us, unto Him be glory in the Church by Christ Jesus throughout all ages, world without end. Amen.

Chapter Five - Intercession

THE distinctiveness of Worship, Confession, and Petition, and their relationship to one another have already been considered. And now we come to the subject of Intercession which rises out of, and rests upon, all that has gone before; and is, in some respects, the most important part of the whole field of Prayer. Let us, then, consider this great subject in some of its many aspects, and first of all —

1. The Ministry of Intercession

(i) *The Essential Principles of Intercession*

If Petition is prayer relative to our personal need, Intercession is prayer relative to the need of others, for we can never intercede on our own behalf. In all intercession at least three persons must always be concerned: the one who speaks, the one spoken to, and the. one spoken for or against. And at least three things must always be presumed: need, on the part of the one spoken of; power, on the part of the one spoken to; and contact with both these persons, on the part of the one who speaks. In Worship, Confession, and Petition there need only be two persons involved, but, let me repeat, in intercession there can never be less than three. A few passages of Scripture may be quoted in support of this.

"Pray not *thou* for *this people,* neither lift up cry nor prayer for them, neither make intercession *to Me,* for I will not hear thee" (Jer. vii. 16).

"*The Lord* turned the captivity of *Job* when he prayed for his *friends*" (ch. xlii. 10).

"Though *Moses* and *Samuel* stood before *Me;* yet My mind could not be towards *this people*" (Jer. xv. 1). "Pray *ye* therefore *the Lord of* the harvest that He will send forth laborers into His *harvest*" (Matt. ix. 38).

In these passages, as the italicized words show, and in scores of passages besides, these two facts are manifest, that at least three must be engaged in this aspect of prayer, and that need, power, and contact, respectively, must be presumed.

Another important fact to bear in mind is that intercession may be *for* or *against* a thing, person, or nation. Here is an illustration of each: "I exhort that intercession be made for all men" (1 Tim. ii. I, 2). "Wot ye not what the scripture saith of Elias? how he maketh intercession to God *against* Israel" (Rom. xi. 2). This ministry may, therefore, be as destructive in one direction as it can be constructive in another; is something to be feared, as well as sought.

The next thing to be regarded is —

(ii) *The Universal Reach of Intercession*

Its arms reach upwards to the throne of grace, and outwards to the ends of the earth. The limit on one side is set, three; but no limit is placed on the other side, short of a whole world, and for all time. Intercession is, perhaps, the most expansive element in prayer on its more active side, for every field of interest which it annexes, opens out to view other and wider fields to be entered and possessed, until the whole world is brought within its province. There is something bracing about inter cession which is not found in petition; something which stirs the soul's deeps, and unfolds its wings, and produces unresting activity in the highest of all services. "Ye that are Jehovah's remembrancers, *take ye no rest, and give Him no rest,* till..." (Isa. lxii. 6, 7). Few, comparatively, exercise the ministry of intercession, but it may be questioned whether any one who has done so ever abandons it. The heart of the intercessor is full, and is enriched and enlarged as it pours itself out for "others." The hands of the intercessor are large, and are ever making great demands upon heaven's supplies for earth's needs. And the eyes of the intercessor are keen and clear; he is a man of vision, a seer, and therefore one who exhibits something of the divine composure, in the face of circumstances which would challenge it.

And this leads to the thought of —

(iii) *The Privilege and Cost of Intercession*

I do not speak at the moment of the duty of prayer in this aspect of it, though that should never be overlooked; but, like so many of our Christian duties, it is also a privilege, and one of the greatest bestowed upon us. That aspect of it to which I would call special attention is the fellowship into which it brings us, and the power with which it entrusts us. And, first of all, it brings us into —

(A) *Fellowship with Christ:* for of Him we read, "He made intercession for the transgressors." "Who also maketh intercession for us." "He ever liveth to make intercession for them." "Christ is entered into heaven itself, now to appear in the presence of God for us." And He said of His present ministry, "I pray for them which Thou hast given Me. Neither pray I for these alone, but for them also which shall believe on Me through their word" (Isa. liii. 12; Rom. viii. 34; Heb. vii. 25, ix. 24; John xvii. 9, 20). The priest hood of Aaron of old was one of intercession; he stood before God on behalf of Israel, and when he went into the Holiest-of-All, he took the atoning blood, and lifted up hands of supplication for the people. Associated with him in this work, but never in the Holiest Place, were the priests. Which things are typical. The Lord Jesus is to-day exercising in heaven the Aaronic Priesthood, that is a Priesthood of Intercession; He has entered into heaven itself, now to appear in the presence of God for us. The priesthoods of Aaron and Melchisedec differed in this, that the hands of the former were uplift towards God in intercession, but the hands of the latter were outstretched to wards the people in benediction. And these two attitudes represent two ages, the present Christian Age of Aaronic Intercession, and the future Millennial Age of Melchisedecan Benediction. The Lord's Aaronic Priesthood in heaven now is being exercised "after the order of Melchisedec," in that there is no succession; but He cannot exercise the Melchisedecan Priesthood until He comes also as King. Christ, then, is interceding in heaven now, and has been doing so without intermission for nearly nineteen hundred years, and in His gracious consideration He has allowed us a glimpse into the nature of that ministry, in His great Intercessory Prayer of John xvii. It would carry us beyond our present purpose to study that prayer carefully here, but two things may be observed. Firstly, that it is on behalf of the Church that Christ is interceding: "I pray not for the world, but for them which Thou has given Me." And, secondly, that His prayer is for our preservation (11), sanctification (17), and unification (21). When Christ was on earth He said, "not My will"; but here, transported in spirit beyond the Cross and the grave, to His Father's right hand, He says "I will that they also whom Thou hast given Me be with Me where I am." He is, there, in the place of authority and power, and is there, exercising a ministry which cannot fail of its end. And we, who are the objects of it, are also taken up into it, and permitted to be sharers with Him in the exercise of it. Had we entered into this privilege from the beginning as we should have done, many a sad chapter in Church History would never have been written. But, late though it be, we may yet enter into this highest and holiest of all fellowships, that of intercession with the risen Christ for His universal Church.

The next part of the privilege is in that we are brought into —

(B) *Fellowship with the Spirit*; for, concerning Him we read, "The Spirit helpeth our infirmities: for we know not how to pray as we ought; but the Spirit Himself maketh intercession for us with groanings which cannot be uttered; and He Who searcheth the hearts knoweth what is the mind of the Spirit, because He maketh intercession for the saints according to the will of God" (Rom. viii. 26, 27). This is a passage which should fill us with wonder and gratitude, for, therein we see that the fullest provision has been made for our varied need in this sphere of life, and as at present constituted. We have an Intercessor above, and we have an Intercessor within. The prayers of Christ, in His perfect humanity, find articulation; but those of the Spirit, through our imperfect humanity, are in groanings which cannot be uttered, but which, we know, are understood and answered.

How intimate and blessed this fellowship with the Spirit is, only they can know who enter into it. Not only does He make intercession for us to God, but also against all that is against us, so that His ministry is both productive and defensive. And He teaches us for what to intercede, and how. He illuminates our understandings, and encourages our hearts, and begets within us something of His own divine passion for the accomplishment of the will of God for the Church and the world. This is our Society in the ministry of intercession, and it should be observed that only in intercession can we have fellowship with Christ and the Spirit in prayer. The Persons of the Godhead do not worship, con fess, or offer thanksgiving, and only in a restricted sense does Christ make petition (John xvii. 24); but in this ministry of good-will and purpose it is given to us to be companions of God. Again, in intercession we are brought into —

(c) *Fellowship with the Saints of all the Ages.* All the great characters of Bible times were great intercessors. How great a man was Moses, scholar, legislator, commander, counsellor, and guide; yet in nothing was he greater, and in no direction did he accomplish more, than in prayer. Study his intercessions recorded in Exod. xvii., xxxii., xxxiii., xxxiv.; Num. xi., xiv., xxi., xxvii.; and then try and estimate how much Israel owed to his prayers. Their very existence depended upon these; and it was only when the people's sin had made it impossible for the Lord to preserve them from judgment, that He said, "Though Moses stood before Me, yet My mind could not be toward this people" (Jer. xv. 1). Samuel is classed with Moses in this matter of power with God in prayer, and at a very critical time in his nation's history his voice prevailed on their behalf (1 Sam. xii.). To what a sublime height did Elijah rise in prayer, when, in the absence of natural evidence he announced the coming rain, and then persisted with God until it came. And among the very greatest of intercessors we must place the Apostle Paul. His habit of life in this respect is clearly set forth in his Letters, wherein we see what a passion he had for men when he stood before God. He says, "God is my witness that without ceasing I make mention of you always in my prayers." "My heart's desire and prayer to God for Israel is that they may be saved." "I thank my God always on your behalf." "My little children, of whom I travail in birth again till Christ be formed in you." "I thank my God upon every remembrance of you, always in every prayer of mine making request for you all with joy." "We do not cease to pray for you." "Night and day praying exceedingly." These utterances represent the passion which flowed through his heart to God in the interests of others; and reflect how much of his time must have been taken up with the ministry of intercession.

To these great names must be added those of Abraham, Ezra, Nehemiah, and Daniel, whose intercessory prayers are models on which our inter cessions might well be framed. Edward VI. prayed with his dying breath that his kingdom might be delivered from the papistry. Tyndale prayed at the stake, "Lord, open the King of England's eyes." The pious Saxon King Oswald, as he expired on the battlefield, prayed, "Spare, Lord, the souls of my people." "I never fail," said the devout Romaine, "to make intercession in all my addresses to the throne of grace." Said an eminent Christian of the seventeenth century, "Always, when you think of your friends, let it be with a praying thought." John Mason, writing to a friend of his, two hundred years ago, said, "Though I have been long silent, I am your orator before the Highest Throne, and do earnestly desire that you may grow in the faith of Jesus, and in lively communion with Him, which is the most comfortable thing in the world."

True intercessors are always great souls, whose passion is well expressed in the words of Samuel Rutherford: "Oh, that Christ would break down the old narrow vessels of these narrow and ebb souls, and make fair, deep, wide, and broad souls, to hold a sea and a full tide, flowing over all its banks, of Christ's love!"

With these, and all others who have held up hands of holy supplication to the God of grace, we are brought into fellowship; our hands are joined with theirs to form an unbroken line right down the ages. God has never left Himself without intercessors, but, alas! how few comparatively, have entered in and stood before Him.

But such work as this costs. Perhaps unwilling ness to pay the price is the reason why so few enter into it. The strenuous and purposeful effort which was put forth by the competitor in the Olympic games, or by the soldier on the field of battle, was put into the prayers of the Apostles and early Christians. Writing to the Galatians, Paul says: "My little children, of whom I am again in *travail* until Christ be formed in you." To the Colossians he writes, "I *strive* for you," that is, of course, in prayer; and the Roman Christians he bids "*strive together*" with him in their prayers to God. Of Epaphras of Colossae we read: "Epaphras saluteth you, always *striving* for you in his prayers, that ye may stand perfect and fully assured in all the will of God"; and not a few have there been since that day, who have exercised a like strenuous ministry, indeed, we have reason to believe that all great movements of the Spirit of God have had their origin in this prayer agony. The wonderful work of grace wrought among the Indians is trace able to the days and nights which Brainerd spent before God in prayer. And this is true of the work accomplished through such men as Jonathan Edwards, Charles G. Finney, and D. L. Moody. But let it not be imagined that this "striving" in prayer is occasioned by unbelief on the part of the sup pliant, or reluctance to bless on the part of God. Wherever there is conflict there is competition or opposition, and this is unquestionably the case in the realm of prayer. There are dark and dangerous forces arrayed against the man who would have power with God in prayer; such an one is challenged at every turn. How remarkable a passage that is in the Book of Daniel in which a mysterious messenger says to the prophet: "Fear not, Daniel: for from the first day that thou didst set thine heart to understand, and to chasten thyself before thy God, thy words were heard, and I am come for thy words. But the prince of the kingdom of Persia withstood me one and twenty days: but, lo, Michael, one of the chief princes, came to help me." The disclosure of this passage is of a be wildering nature, showing us, as it does, something of the power of the spirits of evil to hinder free communication 'twixt heaven and earth; but it reveals the necessity of our "striving" in prayer, not with God, nor with ourselves, but with the powers of evil that are arrayed against God and us. There are values in striving, as we shall see, but the necessity for it lies here. The existence and power of wicked spirits will thus become a very real thing to the intercessor. To-day, these facts are, for the most part, denied or ignored, and that is sufficient explanation of our spiritual impotence. No true man of prayer ever questioned the existence of the devil and his kingdom of evil spirits, because every such one has had to face them on his way to God, and their presence and power have made his prayers intense, with the intenseness of a life-struggle.

Intercession, therefore, must always cost, in time, in thought, in strength, in all that we can give; but it is the price of victory, and not of defeat.

We have only just tapped the subject of Inter cession as a ministry, yet, maybe, enough has been said to show how vast and blessed a ministry it is.

Let us now consider briefly —

2. The Values of Intercession

It may seem strange to speak of Intercession in this way, and yet, it will become obvious, in a moment or two, that this ministry produces an effect upon him who exercises it, scarcely less valuable than that which it accomplishes for and in others. Like every true and gracious outgoing of the soul, the man who prays is doubly blessed, certainly in others, whom his prayers reach; but also in himself, in the act of praying.

What, then, are some of the chief values of this ministry? First of all, I would name —

(i) *The Educative Value of Intercession*

This ministry, rightly understood, cannot be exercised for long without the need being felt of a map, and some knowledge of the world, its peoples, and the history of missionary activity. It may be questioned whether there is any better way of approaching the study of history and geography than from the standpoint of prayer. I am free to confess that my main knowledge of, and chief interest in these have come to me through an awakened sense of what that life and service are, to which we, as believers, are called.

The intercessor must get into the watch-tower, and look out, through cleansed eyes, upon the whole earth; and as he looks he will remember that it is Christ's world and not the devil's. The earth is the field of the redemptive operations, and of our prayer activities. Every great intercessor has been a student of the map. Hudson Taylor pored over China, David Livingstone over Africa, and William Carey over India. These and thousands besides realized that "the field is the world," and that, in order to be effective in service, they must study the "field." Those who have no liking for geography *per se* may, by approaching it from this standpoint, come to be deeply interested in it, and to have a wide and accurate knowledge of it. Europe, Africa, the Americas, Asia, and the Islands of the Seas, will become integral parts of one's stock of thought, and will no longer be distant and unreal. This is our Father's world, and surely we, the children, cannot fail to be interested in the map of our in-heritance. My child said to me recently, "Father, what a lot of geography the present war (1915-16) is teaching me"; and it provoked in me the thought — how much geography the great spiritual conflict of the ages should teach us. We are engaged in a great warfare, and should know where the enemy are gathered in strength, and where their headquarters are. Like Carey, then, we should pray with a map before us, and we shall find that the exercise, incidentally, has a distinctly educative value, and will put us into a new possession of the world in which we live.

What is true of geography, is true also of history. This is a wide and fascinating field of study, into which one may go more or less fully according to ability and time; but it may safely be said that some knowledge of the historic purposes and processes of God, and of the task and progress of Christian Missions, is necessary in order to intelligent intercession. Perhaps the explanation in part, of the lack of intercession on the part of the many is to be found in our ignorance of facts such as would compel prayer. A right historic point of view, and an ever-accumulating stock of facts are indispensable to the truest exercise of intercession. A right point of view can be obtained only by a careful study of the Scriptures; and the facts which give definiteness and reality to our prayers, are to be found in the vast literature concerning the Church and Missions which has grown up during the last hundred years or more. Such facts should be recorded, and made the basis of our supplications.

It must, then, be obvious that intercession has its intellectual and educative values, and that these are by no means to be despised or neglected.

A word or two must be said about —

(ii) *The Human Value of Intercession*

This arises out of the former, and is intimately associated with it. What is human is of interest to us all, and in one sense the dictum of Pope is very true, that "the proper study of mankind is man." Our intercessions will include mankind, and so we must have the peoples before us; the millions in the North, the South, the East, and the West; the countries they live in, the languages they speak; their religions, laws, customs, homes, literature, trades — in short, we shall endeavour to know as much about men everywhere as we can. This brings us into a vast field of investigation, and opens out to view wide possibilities of prayer- service. Such study must destroy the parochialness of ignorance, and set us free from the bondage of petty prejudice. We shall come to look upon men as Christ looks upon them, to see, in some sense, as He sees, and to love, in some measure, as He loves. What we have got to be convinced of is, that souls are souls everywhere, whether the skin be black, or yellow, or white; that souls are all of equal value in God's sight; and that Christ died for all. That conviction will break down all the racial barriers which we have in our pride erected, and will lead us in prayer, and in other ways, to serve all mankind. Have you ever observed how small is the human interest of most Christians? Have we ever attempted to gauge our own? When we have become satisfied as to the fact, then we shall readily see that the cause is ignorance; and perhaps we shall find also, that that ignorance is due, in large measure, to prayerlessness, for, let me repeat, when we come to pray for men, we realize the necessity of knowing some thing about them. Intercession, therefore, has a human value. But there is another, and not the least important of all.

(iii) *The Spiritual Value of Intercession*

What does intercession do for the intercessor? Rather, what does it not do? Prayer is a great discipline, and its exercise contributes very greatly to the work of perfecting which the Spirit is carrying on in the soul. It is the least sensational, and least obtrusive of our spiritual activities; but it is the most important, and the most potent.

Spirituality is the reward of supplication, but not necessarily of any other form of service. A man may preach, and be unreal, but he cannot pray and be unreal, for the prayer that reaches heaven is a work of the Holy Spirit. True prayer begets in the heart love, peace, joy, patience, wisdom, trust, sincerity, courage, and compassion — indeed, all that is divine; so that whatever gains others may derive from our praying, we ourselves are most largely enriched. In intercession we come to know God, and Christ, and the Spirit, and the Bible, and ourselves, and the world, as we could scarcely know them in any other way. Prayer makes the shallow soul deep; the foolish, wise; the ignorant, intelligent; the slothful, busy; the weak, strong; the indifferent, zealous; the un believing, trustful; and the craven, courageous. "More things are wrought by prayer than this world dreams of"; and if only we loved our own souls, we would pray more. Such is the ministry, and such are some of the values of this branch of prayer. There yet remains for our consideration —

3. The Obligation of Intercession

Here let us consider briefly, the need, the supply, and the channel.

In the eleventh chapter of St. Luke's Gospel, our Lord presents the whole case in an incomparable story. He speaks of three friends: one in circumstances of need, one in circumstances of plenty, and one in touch with them both.

"Which of you shall have a friend, and shall go unto him at midnight, and say unto him: Friend, lend me three loaves, for a friend of mine in his journey is come to me, and I have nothing to set before him?"

How simple, yet how significant a story! And as it is uttered in immediate connection with the obligation to pray, it is not difficult to see in these three friends the World and its Need; God and His Supplies; and the Church and her Resources.

Look, then, first at —

(i) *The Human Need*

At least three things are brought to our notice in the short, graphic sentence in which our Lord introduces it.

(a) The Condition of This Friend

He is journeying, passing on, with heavy foot, and burdened heart; and, as the margin of the passage suggests, he is "out of the way," he is off the right track, he is not a pilgrim, but a wanderer, he is lost, and it is midnight. How utterly pitiful is his condition!

Yet there is a picture of the World. It is mid night, and countless millions are wandering on in the darkness, they know not whither, out of the way, they are tramping on, millions in perilous indifference, and millions in dumb despair. Their condition in China, in India, in Africa, in South America, and in Europe is appalling, for they are without God and without hope in the world.

(*b*) The Consciousness of This Friend

"A friend of mine in his journey is come to me." It is then a consciousness of need, for he is "come." He is not wholly ignorant of his real state. Stress of circumstance, bitterest experiences, and voices he has heard in the night, have made him conscious of dark, and cold, and hunger, and the roadless way. But he has seen a light, and has arrived at the house; he is come.

This also is true, perhaps beyond what we imagine, of the world's weary millions. They have been eating, without being satisfied; they have been learning, without coming to know; they have been doing, without any recompense; they have been clothing themselves, and yet are not warm; and they have been hurrying on, but yet have made no progress. And they are awakening to the fact — the consciousness of it all is breaking; and in their despair they are turning to the light that is in Christ, and are coming.

But further, observe —

(*c*) The Claim of This Friend

It is for *bread:* that is what the hungry need. It is for *wine:* that is what the thirsty need; the Bread of Life, and the Wine of the Kingdom. It is also a claim for shelter, and for love; for that is what they need who are in peril, and sore of heart. And this, too, is a picture of the world, for multitudes are learning that religion, and philosophy, and culture, that pleasures and power, and property, are only as husks to the hungry, and the vain promise of life to those who are dying. Remarkable evidence of this is to be found all around us, especially in the Far East, where the dreamy eyes of the Oriental are turning away from their vain hopes and are looking — for what? May we not ask, for Whom?

The wider we read, the better shall we under stand how great is the world's need; and the better we know, the more shall we pray.

But now our attention is directed to —

(ii) *The Divine Supply*

"Which of you shall have a friend and shall go unto him, and say unto him: Friend, lend me three loaves...He will give him as many as he needeth."

The friend who is approached thus, represents God, both by comparison, and by contrast. By comparison, in that it is to Him alone we can appeal for supplies; and in that He gives what we need. And by contrast, in that God is never reluctant to bless the suppliant as the man of this story was. Having regard, then, for the limits of application, these words teach us several great lessons in connection with prayer, and first —

(a) The Divine Supply is Abundant

"He will give him as many as he needeth." This suggests a limitless abundance on the part of the Friend appealed to, which is spoken of else where as "His riches in glory." How sinfully slow we are to learn this truth, revealed on almost every page of Scripture. Our Friend is a God of Pro visions, and with Him is neither limit of store, nor niggardliness of bestowal.

One of the earliest of the names by which He made Himself known to His people was *Shaddai,* always translated, Almighty. "There is some difference of opinion as to the origin or root of the word, but all are pretty well agreed that Shaddai denotes the All-Bountiful One, rather than the Almighty One. *Shad* is the Hebrew for breast, and it is used of the fields, whose manner of be stowing gives us the idea of bounty without wasting or losing their own treasure. The *inexhaustible supply is the essence of the meaning.*" And so we read, "I say unto you . . . He will give him as many as he needeth."

We must never minimize the need of the world; indeed, so great is it that we cannot possibly realize it; yet, could the uttermost be known, it would still be true that in comparison with the supply, it is as a drop to the ocean.

Our prayers for the world's need will be very poor, unless we believe this. We can say with assurance in this connection — what is said of sin and grace in another — "where need abounded, supplies do much more abound."

The next thing to observe is that —

(b) The Divine Supply is Available

The knowledge of stores which are not available, is only a mockery to the hungry. No one who acknowledges that God is, would call into question His limitless resources, but multitudes do not believe that those resources are available. Even among believers this is true, for how many there are, so taken up with the difficulties that attend upon the philosophy of prayer, as never to put it to the proof as a practical power. The Divine sovereignty, natural law, human ignorance, and much besides, are made insuperable difficulties in the way of a practical prayer-life, with the result, that such people never obtain of the divine abundance.

To acknowledge that there is such abundance is not enough; we must be thoroughly convinced that it is available. Selfishness is altogether foreign to the Divine Nature; and the point of the story, so far as this "friend" is concerned, seems to be — if a persistent pleader could arouse so unwilling a friend, how encouraged we should be to come to God, Who is more willing to bless us than we are willing to be blessed.

This leads us to a further truth, namely, that —

(c) The Divine Supply Must Be Appropriated

The abundance, and the availability of it, can bring no comfort to the needy, if it be not applied for, and appropriated. The circulation of blessing is humanly as well as divinely conditioned; and so the second friend comes to the third, on behalf of the first.

Thus we are brought to the final consideration —

(iii) *The Appointed Channel*

We have already said that in intercession, at least three must always be engaged: the one spoken to, the one spoken for, and the one who speaks. They are all here, in these three "friends." There is need at the one end; and supply at the other, and a channel in between, bringing the supply to the need. That is the divine method.

But looking more closely at the subject, one or two things of great importance are brought to our notice, teaching us how we may prevail with God in prayer, on the behalf of others. And first, we mark —

(a) The Sense of Impotence

which possessed this middle friend.

"A friend of mine in his journey is come to me, and *I have nothing* to set before him." A very inadequate knowledge of the extent of the world-need, will drive us to the consciousness — *I have nothing.* As the disciples of old, we look at our poor stores, and say: "What are these among so many?" And well we may. When we try to conceive of the need of the 300,000,000 souls in India; the 400,000,000 in China; and the 180,000,000 in Africa, not to speak of the Americas, and the Continent of Europe, we may well say, "*I have nothing.*" Any idea of ability in us, to cope with this gigantic need, must be based upon a criminal ignorance of the facts of the case. As we read missionary literature, and still more as we travel throughout the world, the consciousness must be driven in upon us that we have nothing. What then shall we do? It is midnight, and our friend, hungry and weary, is making pitiful appeal to us for help. Well, the consciousness of our impotence is the beginning of our power. It is only self- confidence which is finally helpless to grapple with such need. But the awakened believer, or Church, remembers his great Friend, and —

(b) The Secret of Intercession

That is our opportunity, and therein lies our possibilities. To the unspiritual, intercession is regarded as not practical. These believe in public meetings, plenty of organization, endless committees, the spread of literature, and such like, but time spent in prayer is waste time, because it is only talk.

Now do not let us deceive ourselves in this matter. Rightly directed, we cannot have too many of the institutions just named, but without inter cession, these are but as so much cumbersome machinery without any driving power. Prayer is the power-room of all Christian service that is worthy of the name, and if we do not believe that, we shall never accomplish anything, howsoever industrious we may be. Time spent in prayer will yield more than that given to work. Dr. Andrew Murray has said, "If we will but believe in God and His faithfulness, intercession will become to us the very first thing we take refuge in when we seek blessing for others, and the very last thing for which we cannot find time. Between our impotence and God's omnipotence, intercession is the blessed link." Why, then, do we not betake ourselves to prayer?

Practical infidelity is the real reason. But the man of the story, who stands for the Church, or the individual believer, went to his friend and said, "Lend me three loaves." Here is faith, but it is very small, and quite illustrates too many of our requests of God. The divine blessings are not "lent" but given. And it is always well to trust the liberality of God, and not to specify what would barely meet the need. But that which makes this man a model for all intercessors, is —

(c) The Spirit of Importunity

which he manifested.

"He from within answered and said, Trouble me not; the door is shut, and my children are with me in bed; I cannot rise and give thee."

Yet the suppliant who did not obtain by "asking," and "seeking," now begins to "knock." He means to see to it that if his friend will not rise and give him bread, at any rate he shall get no sleep. That is the spirit in which to intercede, and it has the divine warrant and approval, for we are exhorted to take no rest, and give God no rest until the heavenly supplies are secured for the earthly need (Isa. lxii. 6, 7). It is little wonder that we are told—

"Though he will not rise and give him, be cause he is his friend, yet because of his importunity he will rise and give him as many as he needeth."

In this way man may prevail with God, and be the channel of untold blessing to the sin-sick multitudes all around. To exercise this ministry is not only

45

a privilege, it is an obligation, and we shall be held accountable for the neglect of it.

As the Lord Jesus looks down upon us whom He has redeemed, has He to say what He said in the days of long ago?

"I looked, and there was none to help; and I wondered that there was none to uphold."

"I sought for a man among them, that should make up the hedge, and stand in the gap before me for the land, that I should not destroy it: *but I found none.*" Alas, alas, for you and me, if so it be!

An Act of Intercession

By Lancelot Andrewes

> We beseech Thee,
>   remember all, Lord, for good;
> have pity upon all, O Sovereign Lord,
>   be reconciled with us all.
> Give peace to the multitudes of Thy people;
>   scatter offences; abolish wars;
>   stop the uprising of heresies.
>   Thy peace and love
>   vouchsafe to us, O God our Saviour,
> Who art the confidence of all the ends of the earth.
>
> Remember to crown the year with Thy goodness;
>   for the eyes of all wait upon Thee,
> and Thou givest them their meat in due season.
>   Thou openest Thine hand,
> and satisfiest the desire of every living thing.
>
> Remember Thy holy Church,
> from one end of the earth to the other;
>   and give her peace,
>   whom Thou hast redeemed with Thy precious blood;
>   and establish her unto the end of the world.
>
> Remember those who bear fruit, and act nobly, in Thy
>   holy Churches,
> and who remember the poor and needy;
>   reward them with Thy rich and heavenly gifts;
> vouchsafe to them, for things earthly, heavenly,
>   for corruptible, incorruptible,
>   for temporal, eternal.
>
> Remember those who are in virginity,

and purity, and ascetic life;
also those who live in honourable marriage,
  in Thy reverence and Thy fear.

Remember every Christian soul
  in affliction, distress, and trial,
 and in need of Thy pity and succour;
also our brethren in captivity, prison, chains,
  and bitter bondage;
supplying return to the wandering,
  health to the sick,
deliverance to the captives.

 Remember Godfearing and faithful kings,
 whom Thou hast accounted worthy to bear rule upon
   the earth;
especially remember, Lord, our divinely guarded king;
  strengthen his dominion,
subdue under him all adversaries;
speak good things to his heart,
for Thy Church and all Thy people;
vouchsafe to him deep, and undisturbed peace,
  than in his serenity
we may lead a quiet and peaceable life
  in all godliness and honesty.

Remember, Lord, all in power and authority
  and our brethren at court,
 those who are chief in council and judgment,
and all by land and sea waging Thy wars for us.

Moreover, Lord, remember graciously our
   holy fathers,
the honourable presbytery, and all the clergy,
  rightly dividing the word of truth,
and walking uprightly, according thereto.

Remember, Lord, our brethren around us,
 praying with us in this holy hour,
for their zeal and earnestness' sake.

Remember also those who for sufficient cause are away
   and pity them and us
  according to the multitude of Thy mercy.
  Fill our garners with all manner of store,
  preserve our marriages in peace and concord,
  nourish our infants, lead forward our youth,

sustain our aged,
  comfort the fainthearted,
   gather together the dispersed,
restore the wanderers, and knit them to Thy holy
   Catholic and Apostolic Church.

Set free the troubled with unclean spirits,
voyage with the voyagers;
travel with the travellers,
stand forth for the widow,
shield the orphan,
rescue the captive,
heal the sick.

Those who are on trial, in mines, in exile, in galleys,
  in whatever affliction, necessity, and emergency,
       remember, O God;
   and all who need Thy great compassion;
  and those who love us, and those who hate;
    and those who have desired us unworthy
    to make mention of them in our prayers.
All Thy people remember, O Lord, our God,
    and upon all pour out Thy rich pity,
  To all fulfilling their requests for salvation.
  Those of whom we have not made mention
 through ignorance, forgetfulness, or number of names,
do Thou, O Lord, who art the Helper of the helpless,
     The Hope of the hopeless,
   the Saviour of the tempest tossed,
     the Haven of the voyager,
      the Physician of the sick;
do Thou Thyself become all things to all men.
Thou Who knowest each man and his petition,
     each house, and its need.

    Deliver, O Lord, this city,
  and all the country in which we sojourn
   from plague, famine, earthquake, flood,
  fire, sword, hostile invasion, and civil war.
     End the schisms of the Churches,
       quell the ragings of the nations,
    and receive us all into Thy kingdom,
     acknowledging us as sons of light;
        and Thy peace and love
       vouchsafe to us, O Lord our God.

Remember, O Lord our God, all spirits and all flesh

which we have remembered, and which we have not.
    And the close of our life,
    Lord, Lord direct in peace
    to be Christian, acceptable,
  and, should it please Thee, painless,
gathering us together under the feet of Thy chosen,
    when Thou wilt and as Thou wilt,
      only without shame and sin.
The beauty of the Lord our God be upon us;
establish Thou the work of our hands upon us;
  Yea, the work of our hands establish Thou it.

Chapter Six - Thanksgiving

IN our study of the great elements which enter into the making of Prayer, we now come to the fifth and last, Thanksgiving or Praise.

Our Lord's instruction on prayer teaches us that it commences in strict privacy (Matt. vi. 6), and ends in public (Matt, xviii. 20): first, alone with God, and then, before Him in fellowship with others. This is the true order, and can never be interfered with without loss to the one who would pray. The sufficient reason why prayer meetings are so dull, as a rule, is that private prayer is so neglected. If a man is not on intimate terms with God in the secret place, he cannot hope to be powerful and convincing in his public prayers. True intimacy with any one, most of all with God, is not a thing that can be assumed at will: it is the outcome alone of dwelling "in the secret place of the Most High, and abiding under the shadow of Shaddai." And so in our study of Method in Prayer we began with that which was personal and innermost, and have worked to that which, for its highest exercise, perhaps, must be shared with others.

The work of Praise is much wider than that of Worship, in that, while the latter is occupied only with God, the former includes the whole circumference of things of which God is the Centre.

There is a great deal more in the Bible about Thanksgiving or Praise than we would imagine who have paid little attention to the subject; and the great importance of it is everywhere in evidence.

Praise is comely for the upright, therefore His praise should be continually in our mouths. Our tongues should speak of His Praise all the day long, for whoso offereth praise glorifieth Him. We should enter into His courts with praise, for He exalteth the praise of all His saints. It is the Lord Who causeth praise to spring forth, because He delighteth in it: therefore in the midst of the Church we should sing praise. We are to offer the sacrifice of praise continually, that is, the fruit of our lips, giving thanks to His Name.

Let us, then, survey and summarize what the Holy Scriptures have to say on this important matter, in order that we may be instructed of the Lord, how, worthily, to praise Him. In doing so, we shall consider —

1. The Ordinance of Praise.
2. The Occasion of Praise.
3. The Object of Praise.

1. — The Ordinance of Praise

We should remember that —

(i) *Praise is Ordained of God.*

"In everything give thanks, for this is the will of God in Christ Jesus concerning you." "Give unto the Lord the glory due unto His Name." "Whoso offereth praise glorifieth Me." (1 Thess. v. 18; Ps. xxix. 1, 2; 1. 23). These passages, from amongst many, teach us that it is the divine will that we should be praiseful; that praise from us is due to God, and that He is glorified by our praises. How sadly we have forgotten that praise is an obligation as well as a privilege, and that, therefore, there is always occasion for praise. That which God has ordained, He has made possible, not sometimes only, but always; not to some people only, but to all.

David laid hold of this truth, and so was able to say —

> "I will bless the Lord at all times:
> His praise shall continually be in my mouth."

Observe further, that —

(ii) *Praise was Organised in Israel.*

The necessity for method in everything is recognized by all business-like people to-day. But, as a rule, the Christian is most unbusinesslike in the discharge of his spiritual responsibilities. Spiritual service and worship are left, for the most part, to shape themselves, with the result, usually, that they remain for ever shapeless. In these papers on Prayer, I have sought to show how great is the necessity for being methodical in prayer, and what is true of this is true of the whole field of Christian activity. Christian life and service are not going to lose anything of their spirituality by being a great deal more systematic. The soul must be disciplined and cultivated, and these things must not be left to accident or adventure.

Applying this to the subject of Praise, we see that, in Israel, it was not a question of disposition or mood, but of obligation and necessity. Praise in Israel was highly organized.

This organization took place under David, who appointed Twenty- four Courses of Singers (1 Chron. xxv.). The honour of this service fell chiefly to the Levites (1 Chron. xv. 16-22; xvi. 4-6) who led the singing in the Temple Service. But the Levites were by no means the only people who sang, for we read that of the congregation which returned to Palestine under Zerubbabel, "there were among them two hundred singing men and singing women" (Ezra ii. 65). The mention of the women is particularly interesting, as proving their participation in the worship service at that time.

The praise service in Israel was conducted not only by word of mouth, but by many and varied instruments, and must, at any time, have been a most imposing spectacle, and a most inspiring performance.

"It came even to pass, as the trumpeters and singers were as one to make one sound to be heard in praising and thanking the Lord; and when they lifted up their voice with the trumpets and cymbals and instruments of music, and praised the Lord, saying: For He is good; for His mercy endureth for ever; that then the House was filled with a cloud, even the House of the Lord." But we observe further that their —

(iii) *Praise was Ordered in Song.*

Both Old and New Testaments are filled with songs. Indeed, were the praise passages eliminated from the Bible revelation would be so disfigured as to be almost unrecognizable.

(A) Recall some of the songs of praise in the Old Testament. One or two may be named as illustrative of many.

The Song of Moses (Exod. xv.)

This is "the earliest on record of all the sacred odes, and the very foremost in the annals of Hebrew anthology." It has been called Israel's first National Anthem and Te Deum in one. It is their great hymn of emancipation and liberty. It celebrates the deliverance of Israel from Egypt and all the oppression of Pharaoh, and its chief notes are Joy and Victory. The song is sung to the Lord, of the Lord, and for the Lord, and the study of it is quite a liberal education in the art of Praise.

The Song of Deborah (Judg. v.)

This celebrates Israel's great triumph over the Canaanites, and, as the former, is a song to God. Its key-note may be said to be —

"I will sing praise to the Lord."

One of its values is in the way it teaches us to praise God in great detail; to record His dealings with us minutely, and to recite them before Him with gratitude.

The Song of Hannah (1 Sam. ii.)

This is shorter than the two former, but not less precious. It is called a prayer, although there is not a single request in it; and this is incidental evidence that Praise is a part of Prayer, the latter being rightly understood. This song is the Old Testament Magnificat, and its subject is: The Divine Character, 1-3; Method, 4-8; and Aims, 9, 10. It celebrates the Divine goodness in personal experience, as the former songs celebrated that goodness in national experience, and is an incomparable model of praise for every Christian mother.

Of course the Book of Psalms is the great Praise centre of the Bible. It was the Hymn Book of the Hebrew Church, as it has been, in a very true sense, of the Christian Church. The Psalter is perhaps the best known and loved of any part of the Scriptures, and chiefly because it so perfectly reflects our com mon experience.

Calvin has said that "it is a perfect anatomy of the human soul." Its poetry reflects our deepest dejection; and, also, our wildest delight. Worship, Confession, Petition, Intercession, and Thanksgiving are all here, and it is difficult to say which note is dominant.

Within this wonderful collection are three groups of Praise Songs: Psalms ciii.-cvi., cxi.-cxviii., and cxlvi.-cl. In the central group we have what the Jews called the Hallel, which, while the Temple stood, was sung on eighteen days and one night of each year. On the Passover night it was sung in two parts: cxiii. and cxiv. at the beginning of the meal, and cxv.-cxviii. at the end. This is what is referred to in Matt. xxvi. 30.

How full of praise to God are these Psalms! The keyboards of Creation, Providence, and Redemption are all swept by the ecstatic soul; and heaven and earth and sea and sky, things animate and inanimate, are summoned to Praise the Lord.

(B) When we turn to the New Testament, we do not find the songs of the Old dying away, but rising to a climax of ecstasy in the Apocalyptic Choruses. Attention should be given to —

The Songs of Luke

It is not a little significant that only in the Gospel of the Perfect Man do we find these songs recorded, showing how essential a part of perfect human nature Praise is.

The MAGNIFICAT (i. 46-55), is the Virgin's Song of gratitude to God, following the Annunciation of Gabriel. It is intimately related to Hannah's Song, both as to occasion, form, and subject, and is a perfect gem of poetry.

The BENEDICTUS (i. 68-79), is the utterance of Zacharias, both praiseful and prophetic, consequent upon the recovery of his speech, and concerning his newly born son John, the Messiah's forerunner. As in the previous song, it follows closely the Old Testament, in thought and expression.

The GLORIA IN EXCELSIS (ii. 14), is the angelic shout of adoration and benediction whereby the birth of the Messiah and its significance were made known to the shepherds of Bethlehem. This is a song we need to sing in these troublous times, lest we lose sight of the world-peace which is to be when the Messiah comes back again.

The NUNC DIMITTIS (ii. 29-32) is the song of resignation and of revelation which Simeon sang when the long-cherished desire of his heart was fulfilled, and the Appointed of God was actually in his arms in the Temple. It also, in common with all the others, is prophetic, and reaches on to the time when that Babe shall be a "light to lighten the Gentiles, and the glory of His people Israel." Further, in the New Testament, we have a number of —

Sublime Doxologies

A real appreciation of these epitomes of truth and trust would lead us to embody them more frequently in our own praise, both private and public; so let us bring them together for this purpose —

God the Inscrutable

"Oh! the depth of the riches,
  Both of the wisdom and the knowledge of God!
  How unsearchable are His Judgments,
  And His ways past tracing out!
  For, who hath known the mind of the Lord?
  Or, who hath been His counsellor?
  Or, who hath first given to Him
  And it shall be recompensed unto him again?
  For of Him, and through Him, and unto Him
  Are all things. To Whom be the glory for ever.
—AMEN."

God the Self-Revealing

"Now to Him Who is able to stablish you
  According to my Gospel, and the preaching of Jesus Christ;
  According to the revelation of the mystery
  Which hath been kept in silence through times eternal,
  But now is manifested, and by the Scriptures of the prophets —
  According to the commandment of the Eternal God —
  Is made known unto all the nations unto obedience of faith;
  To the only wise God, through Jesus Christ,
  To Whom be the glory for ever. — AMEN."

God the All-Sufficient

"Now unto Him Who is able to do
  Exceedingly abundantly above all that we ask or think,
  According to the power that worketh in us,
  Unto Him be the glory in the Church, and in Christ Jesus,
  Unto all generations for ever and ever. — AMEN."

God the Consummator

"Now unto Him Who is able to guard you from stumbling,
  And to set you before the presence of His glory
  Without blemish in exceeding joy.

"To the only God our Saviour,
Through Jesus Christ our Lord,
Be glory, majesty, dominion, and power,
Before all time, and now, and for ever. — AMEN."

To these must be added the numerous smaller ascriptions of praise, such as are found in Rom. ix. 5; Gal. i. 5; 1 Tim. i. 17; 2 Tim. iv. 18; Heb. xiii. 21; 1 Pet. iv. II; 2 Pet. iii. 18; and Rev. i. 6; and it will be evident how prominent is the note of praise in the music of the New Testament. It would carry us beyond our present purpose to go into the subject of the Liturgy of the Apostolic Church, but there is clear evidence that there was such, of gradual growth, and by Divine sanction and command. Ephes. v. 14 and 18-20 will be a good base from which to study the subject.

The Songs of The Apocalypse

The songs of all the ages are consummated in the grand outbursts of adoration and praise of God which proceed from redeemed creation. Ten thousand times ten thousand, and thousands of thousands, are heard saying with a loud voice —

"Worthy is the Lamb Who was slain
To receive Power, and Riches, and Wisdom,
And Strength, and Honour, and Glory,
And Blessing. Blessing, and Honour
And Glory and Power be unto Him Who sitteth upon the throne,
And unto the Lamb for ever and ever."

And what, very noteworthy, makes these songs so welcome here, is the fact that, for the most part, this is a Book of conflict and of judgment. But it is conflict which issues in the triumph of Christ, and judgment which eventuates in the establishment of truth and justice. It is a veritable Book of "songs in the night," songs which persist until the night for ever departs before the rising of "the Lamb Who is the Light."

Attention must be directed, in the next place, to —

2. — The Occasion of Praise

A study of the foregoing songs will not leave us in any doubt as to what constitutes the great occasions for praise. The countless blessings of which we are the recipients all furnish occasion, but it is impossible to remember and recount them all. Thus, the Psalmist says —

"Bless the Lord, O my soul
And forget not all His benefits."

We well know that the divine mercy outran our best memory, yet we should be for ever blessing the Lord.

From what has been said already, it will not be difficult to classify these countless occasions of thanksgiving to God, though, perhaps, no classification can be exhaustive. We must all sing, first of all—

(i) *The Song of Redemption.*

Most significant is it that, in Scripture, singing is made to begin with the experience of redemption (Exod. xv.). There was no glad song in Israel whilst they were under the oppression of Pharaoh, and the taskmasters' rods. The world may have its music, but with them it is, as Shelley says —

> "The sweetest songs are those that tell
> Of saddest thought."

But that is not true of those who are on the glory side of the Cross. Their mouths are filled with laughter, and their tongues with singing; and their songs are of redemption, deliverance, and forgiveness.

> "Praise, my soul, the King of heaven,
>   To His feet thy tribute bring —
> Ransomed, healed, restored, forgiven,
> Who like thee His praise should sing?
>   Praise Him! Praise Him!
>   Praise the everlasting King."

But, in the next place, ours should be —

(ii) *The Song of Satisfaction.*

The people of Israel were brought out of Egypt to be brought into the land, and if they did not all get there, it was their own fault. He Who redeemed them promised to supply all their need, and guide them through all their days. Like Abram from Ur, when Israel left Egypt they "went forth to go into the land of Canaan," the land of abounding supplies and limitless blessings; but a multitude of them never fulfilled that purpose, and, therefore, were never satisfied. Passage through the Red Sea is the condition of satisfaction, but not its content. In order to the latter, we must get "clean over Jordan" also; and it is we who have believed who enter into that rest, and sing this other song of deep, abiding satisfaction. An acceptance of the work of Christ for us will lead us to sing the song of Redemption, but in order to sing also the song of Satisfaction we must allow Christ to do His sanctifying work in us.

But even this is not all. There must be also —

(iii) *The Song of Victory*

"David spake unto the Lord the words of this song, in the day that the Lord had delivered him out of the hand of his enemies."

There is a very intimate connection between these three songs, and Christian experience is deficient if any of them is missing. Thousands sing the first song who have never learned to sing the other two. They know Christ as the Redeemer, but not as the Satisfier and the Victor. Yet He has promised to satisfy the longing soul, and to fill the hungry soul with goodness. He has promised also to give us power over all the power of the enemy (Ps. cvii. 9; Luke x. 19).

He never intended that our language should be —

"Where is the blessedness I knew
　　When first I saw the Lord?
　Where is the soul-refreshing view
　　Of Jesus and His Word?
　What peaceful hours I once enjoy'd!
　　How sweet their memory still!
　But they have left an aching void,
　　The world can never fill."

How different is this expression of deepest satisfaction with, and completes! victory in the risen Saviour!

"My God, I am Thine, what a comfort divine,
　What a blessing to know that the Saviour is mine.
　In the Heavenly Lamb, thrice happy I am,
　And my heart it doth dance at the sound of His Name."

Praise is not a note, but a chord; not a mere sound, but a harmony; and chief among the notes which make it are Redemption, Satisfaction, and Victory.

The last thought brings us back to the beginning of our subject, to Worship and Adoration.

3. — The Object of Praise

Here we see the cycle of Prayer complete. Worship begetting Confession; Confession begetting Petition; Petition begetting Intercession; Intercession begetting Thanksgiving; and Thanksgiving leading on again to Worship.

God, of course, is the great Object of all true praise; and in the name "God" are included the Three Blessed Persons. This is something to re member which will prove most helpful. We praise the Father, and the Son, and the Spirit, but it is not always desirable to exclude two of the three by naming one, so that, to remember that "God" is inclusive is a real help.

In our praise as in our worship, we think of God according to the ways in which He has manifested Himself which in the main are three. He is —

(i) The God of Creation: Psalm civ.
(ii) The God of Providence: Psalms cv. and cvi.
(iii) The God of Redemption: Psalm ciii.

These ways of manifestation were under consideration in our first study, and so need not be treated again, except to say that in God, and in this three fold revelation of Himself, worship and praise meet, and are one.

I have endeavoured to set forth, only by way of suggestion, the plan of prayer which, for many years, has been more than helpful to myself; and I can only hope and ask that those who read these lines may make better use of the method than I, as yet, have done. In the consideration of such a subject as this we are faced with two perils: the one, the peril of wasting time and effort in our prayer-life, for lack of an understanding of, and method in prayer; the other, the peril of becoming formal and rigid in the employment of a method. If I had to succumb to one or other of these, I would choose the latter; but there is no reason whatever why the adoption of a method in prayer should lead to cold formalism. If man's heart is right, he cannot possibly lose, but gain immensely by the recognition of, and co-operation with, the laws of his mind, based upon an understanding of the wide significance of prayer. Our speeches and sermons are prepared, our hymns are prepared, and the order of our services is prepared; and is there any reason why prayer, which is most important of all, should be left to the inspiration of the moment?

I am not advocating written prayers, but I am urging that we must adopt some true method in prayer, if we are to achieve the most; and although the adoption of the method indicated in this outline may, at first, seem to hamper one's spiritual liberty, it has only to be persisted in, to prove itself of in estimable value, giving definiteness to thought, and economizing time. Only the Spirit of God can teach us how to pray, but to accomplish anything we must learn.

An Act of Thanksgiving

By Lancelot Andrewes

> O Lord, my Lord,
> for my being, life, reason,
> for nurture, protection, guidance,
> for education, civil rights, religion,
> for Thy gifts of grace, nature, worldly goods,
> for redemption, regeneration, instruction,
> for my call, recall, yea, many calls besides;
> for Thy forbearance, longsuffering,
> long longsuffering toward me,

many seasons, many years,
even until now;
for all good things received, successes granted me,
good deeds done;
for the use of things present,
for Thy promise and my hope
of the enjoyment of good things to come;
for my parents honest and good,
teachers kind,
benefactors never to be forgotten,
fellow-ministers who are of one mind,
hearers thoughtful,
friends sincere,
domestics faithful;
for all who have advantaged me
by writings, sermons, conversations,
prayers, examples, rebukes, injuries;
for all these and all others
which I know, which I know not,
open, hidden,
remembered, forgotten,
done when I wished, when I wished not,
I confess to Thee and will confess;
I bless Thee and will bless;
I give thanks to Thee and will give thanks,
all the days of my life.
Who am I, or what is my father's house
that Thou shouldest look upon such a
dead dog as I am?
What shall I render unto the Lord
for all His benefits toward me?
for all things in which He hath spared
and borne with me until now?
Holy, holy holy,
Thou art worthy,
O Lord and our God, The Holy One,
to receive glory, honour, and power:
for Thou hast created all things,
and for Thy pleasure they are
and were created.

Chapter Seven - The Study of Prayer

As studying a picture does not make a man a painter, and as listening to music does not make a man a musician, so reading prayers, and about prayer, will not give a man power with God. And yet as the artist and the musician must study the masterpieces if they would know the power and possibilities of their arts, so the Christian must study prayer if he would be proficient in it. But observe, it is the *artist,* and the *musician,* and the *Christian* who must study. If a man is not an artist or a musician in soul, he may study painting or music all his life, and though he may become accomplished, in a measure, in the technique of these arts, his painting will remain cold, and his music will be passion less. But, given the *Soul* study will be both a necessity and a delight, and will bring one far along the road to perfection. In like manner, an unregenerate person may read about prayer, and study prayers, but such an one can never pray, because that activity belongs only to the awakened and renewed soul. But if spiritual life be possessed, it is both a necessity and obligation that we study the history and principles of prayer, and the great and many models which make our inheritance so rich.

The Corinthian Christians, or some of them, held and acted on the idea that the less νοῦς there was, the more πνεῦμα would there be in the Church; and their error led to the extravagances which the Apostle exposes and rebukes in 1 Cor. xii.-xiv. And are we not in some danger of reviving this error in our time? Is there not a disposition on the part of many believers to think that knowledge is the enemy of zeal, and that activity of the mind curtails the liberty of the heart. Let it be granted that the mind may starve the heart, and that knowledge *may* kill zeal, if mind and knowledge are unsanctified and misdirected. But this they should not be. Paul says, "I will pray with the spirit, and I will pray with the understanding," that is the intellect, the mind (νοῦς). The last thing that we think of putting into prayer is brainsweat, but they who would accomplish most, must apply themselves most. Very far am I from advocating a religious intellectualism which would dry up all emotion; but it is necessary to warn against a religious sentimentalism which is barren of any results.

If we must beware of a "theological undevotion," we must also guard against "an untheological devotion." On this point Bishop Moule has said: "The sentence may be distorted to mean what is absurd. But rightly taken it is a word of truth and wisdom. By 'untheological' is intended what is baseless, un authorized, unreasoned; a 'devotion' which is *careless of its ground* (the italics are mine), its revealed warrant, and also of the true glory of its Object. And the caution has reference to the fact that such 'untheological devotion' has a natural tendency either to evaporate or to degenerate; worship can be kept both pure and warm only by being kept in watchful contact with its true Object and Reason."

These are weighty words, to which we should give most earnest heed. And may I now indicate quite briefly how our devotions may become more "theological," reasoned, and intelligent; how we may build up for ourselves a house of thought in which our spirits shall dwell glad and free?

It will be enough to indicate three lines along which we may study this subject, namely, the life, the laws, and the legacy of Prayer.

I. — The Life of Prayer Reflected in the Bible

We must come to understand that prayer is life, that we are not only to say prayers but to become prayers, as Miss Havergal has said. Prayer is also an outlook, and an atmosphere, of which the Bible in all its parts is ample evidence.

In your study you might divide the Bible into ten periods, and trace throughout each the Life of Prayer. I suggest these periods —

(1) The Beginnings: Adam to Noah.
(2) The Dispersion: Noah to Abram.
(3) The Patriarchal: Abram to Joseph.
(4) The Theocratic: Moses to Samuel.
(5) The Monarchical: Saul to Zedekiah.
(6) The Exilic: The Age of Daniel.
(7) The Restoration: Zerubbabel to Malachi.
(8) The Messianic: The Gospels.
(9) The Apostolic: Acts to Jude.
(10) The Apocalyptic: The Revelation.

To the great men and women who made this wonderful history, prayer was a life. It began, no doubt, in Eden when the sin of our first parents and God's grace towards them were brought home to their consciences. But just outside the gates we find an altar, to which, "at the end of days" (no doubt, the Sabbath, Gen. iv. 3) Cain and Abel brought their offerings. In the same chapter (ver. 26) we read, "Then began men to call upon the name of the Lord." "This first notice is of real importance. There had been abundant consciousness of God before, but tradition fixed the commencement of habitual prayer at the beginning of the third generation." In v. 22 and vi. 9, we read that Enoch and Noah "walked with God," a fellowship which implies an intense prayer-life.

This holy communion between man and God is more evident from the time of Abraham, whose track may be traced by the altars which he built. This is true also, in measure, of Isaac and Jacob. No one could live the life which Joseph did, except by dwelling in the secret place of the Most High and abiding under the shadow of the Almighty. The great souls of this long period of time are the men and women who were "friends of God," and were most at home in His company. To this age belongs Job also, into whose domestic, devotional life we get a glimpse in ch. i. 5 of the drama; who, throughout the time of his terrible sufferings found relief in crying to God, though sometimes the cry was harsh and fierce; and who at the end "prayed for his friends" and secured release from his captivity (xlii. 10). No Biblical life is fuller of prayer than that of Moses. He and Samuel stand out from all others in the divine estimate, as men who had power and could prevail. Thus, when Israel had sinned away the patience and grace of God, He said of them, "Though Moses and Samuel stood before Me, yet My mind could not be towards this people;" and perhaps the distinction of these two was shared by Noah, Daniel, and Job (cf. Ezek. xv. 14).

Not only by the prayers of Moses which are recorded, but from his whole story, we see how entirely his life was a life of prayer, and how very much Israel owed to him on this account. Trace the line of prayer from Moses to Joshua, to Gideon, to Manoah, to Samson, to Hannah, and the prayers of Israel collectively up to the time of Samuel, who, as we have seen, is Moses' brother-soul in intercession, and study this man's life, and then say whether or not the outstanding fact of it was prayer. When Israel clamoured for a king he prayed. When they acknowledged their sin and asked him to speak for them to the Lord, he said, "God forbid that I should sin against the Lord in ceasing to pray for you." On another occasion we read that "he cried unto the Lord all night." His prayers ascended continually to God as incense of a sweet savour. Saul failed because he did not pray. Then we come to David, the organizer of prayer in Israel, and the "man after God's own heart." Study the Psalms, that great Prayer Book of Israel and the Church; it is verily a Book of Common Prayers, reflecting all tempers and circumstances; bitter with sorrow and bright with joy; Calvin well said that "the Collection is a perfect anatomy of the human soul." And all the parts of prayer are here, from Adoration to Thanksgiving; all notes are struck, and all har monies are heard in these incomparable Hebrew Hymns.

Of praying kings must be named with David, Solomon, and Asa, and Jehoshaphat, and Hezekiah, and Josiah. But for these men, and the prophets, the end of Judah had come much sooner; their prayers were the preserving salt in Israel.

Study the life and ministry of the prophets, and you will find that they were essentially men of prayer. They were intercessors in virtue of their calling, taking the needs of men to God, and revealing the mind of God to men. This, in another aspect, was the work of the priest also, and both these offices should be considered in the light of prayer. Cheyne quotes a Rabbinic saying, "In prayer a man should always unite himself with the community," and that is just what both priest and prophet did. Of the latter one has only to think of Samuel, and Elijah, and Elisha, and Amos, and Isaiah, and Jeremiah, and Ezekiel, and Daniel, to realize how great a part prayer played in the life and ministry of a prophet. It would not be an extravagance to say that Israel's continuance de pended on the exercise of it. They who were "sent forth" to the people from God, returned again to report and to intercede. There is much petition in the Old Testament, but more intercession, if the Psalms be excepted. Perhaps this is the case because the unit then was the family rather than the individual.

When we come to the captivity and post captivity periods we see the river of prayer flowing on through the channels of Jeremiah, Ezekiel, Daniel, Ezra, and Nehemiah; and how intensely practical was this ministry may be gathered by studying the Book of Nehemiah. This man was essentially a man of prayer. When he heard bad news of the condition of his people, he prayed. Before he came into the presence of Artaxerxes, he prayed. When his enemies insulted and mocked him, he prayed. When the Jews attempted to thwart his plans, he again turned to God in prayer. It is faith expressed in prayer, and patient, sacrificial toil which have saved the world from precipitate ruin, and of this the Old Testament is proof sufficient.

But when we come to the New Testament fresh light falls upon the whole field of prayer, and new avenues of privilege are opened to us, new principles are revealed, and new possibilities of the prayer- life are disclosed. In the Old Testament prayer was occupied more especially with what is material and temporal, but in the New Testament more largely with what is moral and spiritual. In the former dispensation much of the praying was done by proxy, the priests and prophets being the representatives of the people before God; but in this dispensation there is only "one Mediator between God and men, the man Christ Jesus." Formerly the Holy Spirit came only upon some, and permanently in dwelt none; but now He *for ever* indwells *every* believer so that all may "come boldly to the throne of grace." These, and other distinctions between the two dispensations in relation to the subject of prayer should be traced.

How sublime and strong a thing is the prayer- life m the New Testament. The example of our Lord is, of course, superlative. Collect all references in the Gospels which reflect this aspect of His life, and study the setting of each; such expressions, for instance, as these —

"He withdrew Himself into the wilderness and prayed."

"In those days He went out into a mountain to pray, and continued all night in prayer to God."

"It came to pass as He was alone praying."

"About eight days after these sayings He went up into a mountain to pray. And as He prayed the fashion of His countenance was altered."

"It came to pass as He was praying in a certain place."

"In the day time He was teaching in the Temple; and at night He went out and abode in the mount that is called the Mount of Olives."

"Judas who betrayed Him, knew the place, for Jesus ofttimes resorted thither."

"On the morrow (morning), when they were come from Bethany, He was hungry." He had not breakfasted. Why?

This is a rich field of inquiry, and when we attempt to realize Who it is Who found prayer to be such a necessity, we surely shall be shamed out of our own prayerlessness.

Passing on to the Apostolic Church, we see in both the History of the Letters that when the early Christians were most prayerful they were most powerful, and that with a less firm hold upon God in Christ their love declined and their influence waned.

Luke must himself have been a man of much prayer, and as an historian, in his two books he seizes upon the internal and vital in the life of our Lord and of the Church, rather than upon what was out ward and accidental, that is, he gives special attention to the working of prayer.

There is definite reference to this subject in nearly every chapter of the Acts, the atmosphere of prayer pervades the whole book. The Letters, which should be interwoven with the History, present the same high level of life, not always as realized, but always as possible and to be pursued.

Christ's greatest Apostle was a man of prayer unceasing, and makes frequent reference to his inter cessions and supplications. The prayers of Paul constitute an ample subject for study, and much that is helpful has been written thereon. James, also, urges the necessity of prayer; and the fragrance of John's own inner life is something that is felt in his books.

There is much in the Apocalypse about prayer, and, as befits the place assigned to it at the end of the Canon, the Book "ends with a prayer from the highest level of Christian faith and hope."

Thus does this silvery stream, rising in the Garden of Eden, flow on in ever-increasing strength and beauty until it enters the Holy City in the regained Paradise of God, where as praise, if not as supplication, it is a source of un-failing delight both to God and the redeemed.

We should turn our attention next to —

2. — The Laws of Prayer Revealed in The Bible

The working of prayer is as definitely conditioned as the operations of nature, and we must know what these conditions are, and be subject to them if we would pray effectually. Prayer is not a leap in the dark, or a beating of the air, but a science in which cause and effect work with precision, and in which promise and performance have a fixed relation.

It is something little short of mockery for us to beseech God to fulfil to us His promises, while we are wilfully disregarding the conditions on which they rest. How often have we heard the cry, "Lord, open Thou the windows of heaven and pour us out such a blessing that there shall not be room to receive it." But how very rarely have we heard the confession, "Lord, I now bring into the storehouse the whole tithe." Yet, read the passage —

"Bring ye all the tithes into the storehouse, that there may be meat in Mine house, and prove Me now herewith, saith the Lord of hosts, if I will not open you the windows of heaven, and pour you out a blessing, that there shall not be room enough to receive it."

If we obey the precept, He will fulfil the promise; and until we do obey, let us cease to claim the promise.

"If I regard iniquity in my heart the Lord will not hear me." That is plain enough for any child to understand, and yet, so insensible are many of the force and finality of the words that they persist in asking God for His blessing while living in known sin. To do this is itself a terrible sin, for it is fool ing with God; and the prayers of the backsliding Christian are worse than waste of breath.

Just because prayer is conditioned all prayers are not answered, and Scripture is quite perspicuous on this point. Where prayer is hypocritical there is no answer —

"When thou prayest, thou shalt not be as the hypocrites: for they love to pray standing in the synagogues and in the corners of the streets, that they may be seen of men. Verily, I say unto you, They have their reward" (when they are seen of men).

Where prayer is formal or perfunctory there is no answer —

"When ye pray, use not vain repetitions, as the heathen do, for they think that they shall be heard for their much speaking."

Where prayer is a substitute for action there is no answer —

"Joshua said, Alas, O Lord God, wherefore hast Thou at all brought this people over Jordan, to deliver us into the hands of the Amorites, to destroy us? would to God we had been content, and dwelt on the other side of Jordan!

"And the Lord said unto Joshua, Get thee up; wherefore liest thou thus up- on thy face? Israel hath sinned...Thou canst not stand before thine enemies, until ye take away the accursed thing from among you; neither will I be with you any more, except ye destroy the ac cursed thing from among you."

To make prayer a substitute for performance is to violate one of its laws, and so to render it un availing. I have heard of a domestic who asked her minister if he would pray for her that she might get up when the alarum rang in the morning; and he replied: "Certainly I will not; all you have to do is to put your feet on the floor."

Where desire and motive are carnal, prayer is not answered —

"Ye ask and receive not, because ye ask amiss, that ye may consume it upon your lusts."

Where the Divine Will is set aside prayer is not answered —

"Ye shall cry out in that day because of your king which ye shall have cho- sen you; and the Lord will not hear you in that day."

Where there is unbelief, prayer is not answered —

"He that wavereth is like a wave of the sea driven with the wind and tossed. Let not that man think that he shall receive anything of the Lord, a double-minded man, unstable in all his ways."

We have already seen that where sin is cherished prayer is not answered, and there are many other grounds of denial revealed in Scripture, which we should seek out in order to avoid. But the larger side of the subject is practical and positive. The Bible abounds in exhortations to prayer, and the conditions which lead to a right exercise of it are amply set forth.

It may start some young Christian along a line of most fruitful research to find a text or texts in support of each of the following twenty-one points —

Prayer must be to God (   ) . In the name of Jesus (   ). By the aid of the Spirit (   ). According to the Divine Will (   ). It must be in secret (   ); and collective (   ). Also, Definite (   ). Sincere (   )'. Believing (   ). Sacrificial (   ). Unceasing (   ). Importunate (   ). Strenuous (   ). Humble (   ). Patient (   ). For things Spiritual (   ), and Temporal (   ). Intelligent (   ). Watchful (   ). Joyful (   ). Effectual (   ).

If these, and many other conditions are observed by us in our practice of prayer, we assuredly shall be "neither barren nor unfruitful" in this holy ministry.

Precept and promise are vitally related in the divine covenant, and "what God hath joined together let no man put asunder." If we obey, God will operate: if we believe, He will bless; if we follow Him, He will fulfil His word to us. Let us then come boldly to the throne of grace, which is the throne of the divine government, and there prove Him, Who has permitted and bidden us so to do.

In closing, we may well think of —

3. — The Legacy of Prayer Recorded in the Bible

On this aspect of our subject it would be easy to write a long chapter, but I forbear. Let me, however, recommend to the reader of these pages that you work through the Bible from the beginning, gathering out all the prayers which, in the providence of God, have been preserved through the ages. There are not a few of considerable length; and there are scores of shorter prayers. It would be well to classify these, with reference to the Author, the Age, the Circumstances, the Substance, the Structure, and the Effect of each. Only when this is done shall we be in a position to measure and appreciate the wealth of devotional material which is at our disposal for constant inspiration and use.

Think, for example, of the Colloquy of Abram and Jehovah over Sodom and Gomorrah (Gen. xviii.), and of Moses and Jehovah about the deliverance of Israel from Egyptian bondage (Exod. iii., iv.); of David's song of praise in the day that the Lord delivered him out of the hands of all his enemies (2 Sam. xxii.); of Solomon's great prayer at the dedication of the Temple (1 Kings viii.); of Daniel's confession, and Ezra's and Nehemiah's, of the sins of their people in the ninth chapter of the books bearing their names. Think also, of Isaiah's earnest pleadings (chs. lxiii. 7 to lxiv. 12); and Jeremiah's lamentations (Lam.). Coming to the New Testament, let us remember our Lord's great intercessory prayer (John xvii.); and the prayer which He taught His disciples (Matt, vi.); and the prayers of Paul found in his Epistles to the Churches. If these were all we possessed we would be wealthy indeed, but we have innumerable smaller prayers scattered from Genesis to Revelation, prayers of Abram, and Lot, and Eliezer, and Isaac, and Jacob, and Job, and Moses, and Israel, and Joshua, and Gideon, and Samson, and Hannah, and Samuel, and David, and Korah, and Ethan, and Asaph, and Elijah, and Joel, and Jonah, and Amos, and Isaiah, and Hezekiah, and Habakkuk, and Nehemiah. And in the New Testament there are prayers of our Lord, and of His Apostles; of the martyred saints in the Apocalyptic vision; and of the redeemed and glorified in heaven. To this enormous heritage must be added numberless prayers of the saints of the Christian Era from the first age of martyrdom down to the present day. When all this is considered, we shall be compelled to acknowledge that if we have failed in prayer, it has been largely due to ignorance or sloth. Let that, however, be true no longer, but let us arise and "possess our possessions."

www.ingramcontent.com/pod-product-compliance
Lightning Source LLC
Chambersburg PA
CBHW032030040426
42448CB00006B/788